THE CHRIST
OF INDIA

THE CHRIST OF INDIA

The Story of Original Christianity

SWAMI NIRMALANANDA GIRI
(ABBOT GEORGE BURKE)

LIGHT OF THE SPIRIT
PRESS
CEDAR CREST, NEW MEXICO

Published by
Light of the Spirit Press
lightofthespiritpress.com

Light of the Spirit Monastery
P. O. Box 1370
Cedar Crest, New Mexico 87008
OCOY.org

ISBN-13: 9780998599847

Library of Congress Control Number: 2017955502
Light of the Spirit Press, Cedar Crest, New Mexico

BISAC Categories:
1. REL006710 RELIGION / Biblical Studies / Jesus, the Gospels & Acts
2. OCC031000 BODY, MIND & SPIRIT / Ancient Mysteries
   & Controversial Knowledge
3. OCC012000 BODY, MIND & SPIRIT / Mysticism

Second Edition, May 2018

07152023

CONTENTS

PREFACE

"Original Christianity" is the teaching of both Jesus of Nazareth and his Apostle Saint Thomas in India. But although it was new to the Mediterranean world, it was really the classical, traditional teachings of the ancient rishis of India that even today comprise Sanatana Dharma, the Eternal Dharma, that goes far beyond religion into actual realization through the practice of yoga. (See Appendix Two: The Yoga of the Nath Yogis and Jesus.) The material in this book will reveal that this statement is simple fact without exaggeration.

Jesus and the Apostle Thomas taught nothing new in either Israel or India. Their religion was identical with that which Jesus studied in India, that which is found in the Upanishads, the Bhagavad Gita and other fundamental scriptures and spiritual writings of India. Jesus and Saint Thomas taught nothing but Sanatana Dharma. The deformed entity known today as "Christianity" is a corruption and betrayal of their actual teachings. Jesus learned his wisdom from the sages of India and so must those who would follow him.

I am not the originator of this idea. In 1920 Swami (later Paramhansa) Yogananda came to America to speak at a religious conference in Boston, Massachusetts. In his discourse at that conference he announced that he would be remaining in America and giving weekly classes of one and a half hours in length: the first half hour would be on the teachings of the Bhagavad Gita, the second on the teachings of the Gospels, and the third on the fundamental unity of the two. For thirty-two years he held to this approach. Today many people in East and West carry on that vision. I am just one of them.

t Those who would follow Christ in all honesty will eventually find themselves following him to India.

> *Note:* I wish to apologize that many quotations in this book have no attribution. Much of the material presented in the sections "The Christ of India" and "The Apostle of India" was gathered from books which I found in both North and South India, printed by the Indian Society For The Propagation of Christian Knowledge, the Roman Catholic Church and the Saint Thomas Church. I put it all in typewritten form just for my personal use without noting where it came from, not foreseeing the very real need for complete documentation in case one day I might want to print some or all of it.

Throughout the text are references to articles which may be found on our website, www.OCOY.org.

THE CHRIST OF INDIA

Essene roots of Jesus

At the time of Jesus there were two major currents or sects within Judaism: the Pharisees and the Sadducees. The Pharisees were extremely concerned with strict external observance of their interpretation of the Mosaic Law, ritual worship and theology. The Sadducees, on the other hand, were very little concerned with any of these things and tended toward a kind of genteel agnosticism. Today these two groups might be compared with the Orthodox and the Reformed branches of Judaism respectively.

There was a third sect which both was and was not part of Judaism. They were the Essenes, whose very name means "the Outsiders." "Essene" is the Greek equivalent of the Hebrew *Chitsonim*, "the outsiders." Since Philo and other Jewish historians used "Essene" in writing about them, that has become the common usage. Whether they chose this name for themselves or whether it was applied to them by the disdainful Pharisees and Sadducees is not known. But that they were incongruent (even incompatible) to the normal life of Israel at that time is certainly known.

Jesus of Nazareth was an Essene, as were most of his followers, including the twelve Apostles (some of whom were his cousins). Many elements distinguished and even separated the Essenes from the rest of Israel.

Their claims about their very existence was certainly a controversial matter. For the Essenes averred that Moses had created them as a secret fraternity within Judaism, with Aaron and his descendants at their head. The prophet Jeremiah was a Master of the Essenes, and it was in his lifetime that they ceased to be a secret society and became a public entity. From that time many of the Essenes began living in communities. Isaiah and Saint John the Baptist were also Masters of the Essenes.

Their purpose was to follow a totally esoteric religious philosophy and practice that was derived from the Egyptian Mysteries. As the grandson of the Pharaoh, Moses had been an initiate of those mysteries and destined to ultimately become the head of the Egyptian religion. It was common in Egypt for the eldest son of the Pharaoh to inherit the throne, and the next eldest son to be made the head of the Egyptian religion. Although Moses was the only son of the Pharaoh's daughter, he was adopted and his bloodline was not known. For this reason he could not be Pharaoh, but he could be put into the position usually given to the second son. The Egyptian Mysteries were themselves derived from the religion of India, as was openly admitted when Apollonius of Tyana publicly debated the officials of the Egyptian religion who censured him for having studied in India and brought those teachings back to the Mediterranean world.

Because of this, the Essenes had always maintained some form of contact and interchange with India—a fact that galled their fellow Israelites. Regarding this, Alfred Edersheim, in his nineteenth century classic, *The Life and Times of Jesus the Messiah*, wrote: "Their fundamental tendency was quite other than that of Pharisaism, and strongly tinged with Eastern elements."

The reality of this contact with India is shown in the *Zohar* (2:188a-b), a compilation of ancient Jewish mystical traditions and the major text of the Jewish Kabbalah. It contains the following incident regarding the knowledge of an illumined rabbi concerning the religion of India and the Vedic religious rite known as the sandhya, which is an offering of prayers at dawn and sunset for enlightenment.

"Rabbi Yose and Rabbi Hiyya were walking on the road. While they were walking, night fell; they sat down. While they were sitting, morning began to shine; they rose and walked on. Rabbi Hiyya said, 'See, the face of the East, how it shines! Now all the children of the East [in India], who dwell in the mountains of light [the Himalayas], are bowing down to this light, which shines on behalf of the sun before it comes forth, and they are worshipping it.... Now you might say: 'This worship is in vain!' but since ancient, primordial days they have discovered wisdom through it."

Their contact and interchange with Indian religion—Brahminical practices in particular—were manifested in several ways among the Essenes:

1. They practiced strict non-violence.

2. They were absolute vegetarians and would not touch alcohol in any form. Nor would they eat any food cooked by a non-Essene. Edersheim says: "Its adherents would have perished of hunger rather than join in the meals of the outside world."

3. They refused to wear anything of animal origin, such as leather or wool, usually making their clothes of linen.

4. They rejected animal sacrifice, insisting that the Torah had not originally ordered animal sacrifice, but that its text had been corrupted in regard to that and many other practices as well. Their assertion was certainly corroborated by passages in the scriptures such as: "Will I eat the flesh of bulls, or drink the blood of goats?" (Psalms 50:13). "To what purpose [is] the multitude of your sacrifices unto me? saith the Lord:... I delight not in the blood of bullocks, or of lambs, or of he goats" (Isaiah 1:11). "For I spake not unto your fathers, nor commanded them in the day that I brought them out of the land of Egypt, concerning burnt offerings or sacrifices" (Jeremiah 7:22). The quotations from Isaiah and Jeremiah are particularly relevant since they were themselves Masters of the Essenes.

It was the Essenes' contention that the "animals" originally offered in sacrifice were symbolic effigies of animals that represented the particular failing or fault from which the offerer wished to be freed. Appollonius of Tyana taught this same thing in relation to the ancient Greek sacrifices, and urged a return to that form. Long before that, in India dough effigies were offered in "sacrifice." (See page 42 of *Ganesha*, by Chitralekha Singh and Prem Nath, published by Crest Publishing House of New Delhi.) In the Essene practice, each person molded the effigies himself while praying and concentrating deeply on the traits he wished to have corrected, feeling that they were being transferred into the image. The effigies were made of five substances: powdered frankincense, flour, water, olive oil, and salt. When these had dried, they were taken to their tabernacle whose altar was a metal structure with a grating over the top and hot coals within. The effigies were laid upon this grating and burnt by the intense heat. As they burned, through the force of the heat the olive oil and frankincense liquefied and boiled or seeped up onto the surface of the figure. This fragrant liquid was called "the blood" of the sacrifice. The Essenes contended that it was this liquid with which Moses consecrated the tabernacle, its equipment, and the priests (Exodus 24:6, 8), not animal blood. And it was just such a "lamb" whose "blood" was sprinkled on the doorposts in Egypt (Exodus 12:7).

For the Passover observance, the Essenes would bake a lamb effigy using the same ingredients, except for the frankincense they would substitute honey and cinnamon. (Or, lacking honey, they would use a kind of raisin syrup.) This was the only paschal lamb acceptable to them—and therefore to Jesus and his Apostles.

Consequently, the Essenes refused to worship in Jerusalem, but maintained their own tent-tabernacle on Mount Carmel made according to the original directions given to Moses on Mount Sinai. They considered the Jerusalem temple unacceptable because it was a stone structure built according in Greco-Roman style rather than the simple and humble tabernacle form given to Moses—a form that symbolized both the physical and psychic makeup of the human being. Further, the Jerusalem temple was built by Herod who, completely subservient to Rome, disdained Judaism and practiced a kind of Roman agnostic piety. Because of this the temple was ritually unclean in their estimation. They placated the Jerusalem Temple priests by sending them large donations of money. On occasion they gave useful animals to the Temple in Jerusalem, but only with the condition that they would be allowed to live out their natural span of life.

5. They interpreted the Torah and other Hebrew scriptures in an almost exclusively spiritual, symbolic and metaphysical manner, as did the Alexandrian Jewish philosopher Philo. They also had esoteric writings of their own which they would not allow non-Essenes to see. But even more objectionable to the other Hebrews was their study and acceptance of "alien" scriptures–the holy books of other religions–so much so that an official condemnation was made of this practice. In light of this we can say that the Essenes were perhaps the first in the West to hold a universal, eclectic view of religion.

6. Celibacy was prized by them, being often observed even in marriage, and many of them led monastic lives of total renunciation.

7. They considered their male and female members–all of whom were literate–to be spiritual equals, and both sexes were prophets and teachers among them. This, too, was the practice in Hinduism at that time, women also wearing the sacred thread (yajnopavita).

8. They denied the doctrine of the physical resurrection of the dead at the end of time, which was held by the Pharisees and later became a tenet of Mediterranean Christianity.

9. They believed in reincarnation and the law of karma and the ultimate reunion of the soul with God. This is clearly indicated by the Apostles asking Jesus about a blind man: "Master, who did sin, this man, or his parents, that he was born blind?" (John 9:2. See *May a Christian Believe in Reincarnation?*).

10. They believed that the sun was a divine manifestation, imparting spiritual powers to both body and mind. They faced the rising and

setting sun and recited prayers of worship, refusing upon rising in the morning to speak a single word until the conclusion of those prayers. They did not consider the sun was a god, but a symbol of the One God of Light and Life. It was, though, felt that appropriate prayers directed toward the sun would evoke a divine response. (See Jesus' words to the king of Kashmir as recorded in the *Bhavishya Maha Purana* that are given later on.)

11. They believed in both divination and the powers of prophecy.

12. They believed in the power of occult formulas, or mantras, as well as esoteric rituals, and practiced theurgy (spiritual "magic") with them.

13. They believed in astrology, cast horoscopes, and made "magical" amulets of plants and gems according to astrological aspects. They also believed that angels had taught Moses the practice of herbalism.

14. They believed that miraculous cures were natural extensions of authentic spiritual life.

15. They would wear only white clothes as a sign that they worshipped God who is Light and were clothed by him in light. This so provoked the other Israelites that praying in white clothing was prohibited by the Pharisees and Sadducees, and laws were drafted accordingly. (The Mishnah *begins* with such a prohibition.) The disciples of Saint Thomas in India had a similar rule, only wearing white clothes in worship.

16. They observed the identical rules of purity (shaucha/shuddhi) as the Brahmins in India at that time, especially in the matter of bathing frequently.

17. They practiced the strictest adherence to truthfulness. (Travelers in past centuries cited the strict adherence to truth by the Brahmins of India as a great and admirable wonder.)

So it is not out of place to consider that the Essenes—and Jesus and his disciples—possessed the qualities of Hindu religion in "the West" at that time.

From all this we can see why Edersheim states that "In respect of doctrine, life, and worship, it [the Essene community] really stood *outside* Judaism." As a result of these differences from ordinary Judaism, the Essenes lived totally apart from their fellow Hebrews, usually in separate communities or in communal houses in the towns and cities. (The supposed "communal experiment" in the book of Acts (4:32) was really a continuation of the Essene way of life. The Last Supper took place in just such an Essene "house.")

The history of Isha–Jesus the Christ

Among the Essenes of Israel at the threshold of the Christian Era, none were better known or respected than Joachim and Anna of Nazareth. Joachim was noted for his great piety, wealth and charity. The richest man in Israel, his practice was to annually divide his wealth into three parts, giving one to the temples of Carmel and Jerusalem and one to the poor, keeping only one part for himself. Anna was renowned as a prophetess and teacher among the Essenes. Their daughter Mary [Miryam], who had been conceived miraculously beneath the Holy of Holies of the Temple (see *The Unknown Lives of Jesus and Mary*), had passed thirteen years of her life as a Temple virgin until her espousal to Joseph of Nazareth. Before their marriage was performed, she was discovered to have conceived supernaturally, and in time she gave birth to a son in a cave of Bethlehem. His given name was Jesus (Joshua: Yeshua in Aramaic and Yahoshua in Hebrew).

This son of Miryam was as miraculous as his mother, and astounding wonders were worked and manifested daily in his life–for the preservation of which his parents took him into Egypt for some years where they lived with various Essene communities there. But before that flight, when the child had been about three years old, sages from India (Matthew 2:1-2) had come to pay him homage and to establish a link of communication with him, for his destiny was to live most of his life with them in the land of Eternal Dharma before returning to Israel as a messenger of the very illumination that had originally been at the heart of the Essene order. Through the intermediary of merchants and travelers both to and from India, contact was maintained with their destined disciple.

At the age of twelve, during the passover observances on Mount Carmel (not in Jerusalem), Jesus petitioned the elders of the Essenes for initiation–something bestowed only on adults after careful instruction and scrutiny. Because of his well-known supernatural character, the elders examined him before all those present. Not only could he answer all their questions perfectly, when the examination was ended he began to examine *them*, putting to them questions and statements that were utterly beyond their comprehension. In this way he demonstrated that the Essene order had nothing whatever to teach him, and that there was no need for him to undergo any initiation or instruction from them.

Upon his return to Nazareth preparations were begun for his journeying into India to formally become a disciple of those masters who had come to him nine years before. The necessary preliminaries being completed, Jesus set forth on a spiritual pilgrimage that would end at the feet of the three masters who would transform Jesus the Nazarene into Isha the Teacher of Dharma and Messiah of Israel. Nicholas Roerich, in his book *Himalaya: A Monograph*, said that according to the Tibetan scrolls he found in 1925, Isha was thirteen when he left for India. The *Nathanamavali* of the Nath Yogis, which we will be considering later on, says that Isha reached India when he was fourteen.

The spiritual training of Jesus

In India the masters instructed Jesus in yoga and the highest spiritual philosophy, giving him the spiritual name "Isha," which means Lord, Master, or Ruler, a descriptive title often applied to God (Ishwara). It is also a title of Shiva.

For some time Jesus meditated in a cave north of the present-day city of Rishikesh, one of the most sacred locales of India.

This is the cave north of Rishikesh in which Jesus lived for some time. In the last century both Swami Rama Tirtha and Swami (Papa) Ramdas lived there (at separate times), and had visions of Jesus meditating there, though they had no prior knowledge of his having lived there.

Varanasi (Benares)

Jesus also lived for some time in Benares, the sacred city of Shiva, the formless Absolute. The worship of Shiva centered in the form of the natural elliptical stone known as the Shiva Linga (Symbol of Shiva) was a part of the spiritual heritage of Jesus, for his ancestor Abraham, the father of the Hebrew nation, was a worshipper of that form. The Linga which he worshipped is today enshrined in Mecca within the Kaaba. The stone, which is black in color, is said to have been given to Abraham by the Archangel Gabriel, who instructed him in its worship.

Such worship did not end with Abraham, but was practiced by his grandson Jacob, as is shown in the twenty-eighth chapter of Genesis. Unwittingly, because of the dark, Jacob used a Shiva Linga for a pillow and consequently had a vision of Shiva standing above the Linga which was symbolically seen as a ladder to heaven by means of which devas (shining ones) were coming and going. Recalling the devotion of Abraham and Isaac, Shiva spoke to Jacob and blessed him to be an ancestor of the Messiah. Upon awakening, Jacob declared that God was in that place though he had not realized it. The light of dawn revealed to him that his pillow had been a Shiva Linga, so he set it upright and worshipped it by pouring oil over it, as is traditional in the worship of Shiva, naming it (not the place) Bethel: the Dwelling of God. (In another account in the thirty-fifth chapter, it is said that Jacob "poured a drink offering thereon, and he poured oil thereon." This, too, is a traditional form of worship and offering in India.) From thenceforth that place became a place of pilgrimage and worship of Shiva in the form of the Linga stone. Later Jacob had another vision of Shiva, Who told him: "I am the God of Bethel, where thou anointedst the pillar, and where thou vowedst a vow unto me" (Genesis 31:13). A perusal of the Old Testament will reveal that Bethel was the spiritual center for the descendants of Jacob, even above Jerusalem. So it would not be without basis to conclude that Original Judaism also was Sanatana Dharma.

Although this tradition of Shiva [Linga] worship has faded from the memory of the Jews and Christians, in the nineteenth century it was evidenced in the life of the stigmatic Anna Catherine Emmerich, an Augustinian Roman Catholic nun. On several occasions when she was deathly ill, angelic beings brought her crystal Shiva Lingas which they had her worship by pouring water over them. When she drank that water she would be perfectly cured. Furthermore, on major Christian holy days she would have out-of-body experiences in which she would be taken to Hardwar, a city sacred to Shiva in the foothills of the Himalayas, and from there to Mount Kailash, the traditional abode of Shiva, which she said was the spiritual heart of the world. (See the two-volume *Life of Anna Katherina Emmerich* by Karl Schmoger.)

Jagannath Puri

Jesus lived for a while in Jagannath Puri, which at that time was a great center of the worship of Shiva, second only to Benares. In Puri Jesus lived some time in the famous Govardhan Math, today a major center of the monastic order of the foremost philosopher-saint of India known as Adi Shankaracharya.

In the nineteen-fifties, the former head of the Govardhan Math, and senior figure of the entire monastic Swami Order of Shankaracharya, Jagadguru Bharati Krishna Tirtha, claimed that he had discovered "incontrovertible historical evidence" that Jesus had lived in the Govardhan Math as well as in other places of India. He was writing a book on the subject, but died before it could be finished. Unfortunately the fate of his manuscript and research is presently unknown.

The guru of Paramhansa Yogananda, Swami Sri Yukteswar Giri, had an ashram in Puri and he, too, wrote a book proving that Jesus had lived in India and been a teacher of Sanatana Dharma. (Perhaps he had access to the same material the Shankaracharya later found.) A missionary asked to borrow it and never returned it. After the passing of Sri Yukteswar his disciples asked for the return of the book but the missionary denied ever having it.

Return to the West

During the years he lived in India Jesus visited many spiritual centers both Hindu and Buddhist, including some in Ladakh as will be seen later, then set forth on his return journey to Israel with the blessings of the masters. Jesus was aware of the form and purpose of his life and temporary death from his very birth. But it was the Indian masters who made everything clear to him regarding them. They promised Jesus that he would be sent a container of Himalayan Balsam to be poured upon his head by a close disciple as a sign that his death was imminent, even "at the door." When Saint Mary Magdalene performed this action in Bethany, Jesus understood the unspoken message, saying: "She is come aforehand to anoint my body to the burying" (Mark 14:8).

All along his way, especially in Persia, Jesus taught those who were drawn to his spiritual magnetism and who sought his counsel in the divine life. Arriving in Israel, he went directly to the Jordan where his cousin John, the Master of the Essenes, was baptizing. There his Christhood was revealed to John and those who had "the eyes to see and the ears to hear" (Matthew 3:13-17). In this way his brief mission to Israel was begun. Its progress and conclusion are well known, so we need not recount it here except to rectify one point.

Misunderstanding becomes a religion

Throughout the Gospels we see that the "Western" disciples of Jesus consistently misunderstood his speaking of higher spiritual matters. When he spoke of the sword of wisdom they showed him swords of metal to assure him they were well equipped (Luke 22:36-38). When he warned them against the "leaven" of the Scribes and Pharisees they thought he was complaining that they did not have any bread (Mark 8:15-16). Is it any wonder, then that he said to them: "Perceive ye not yet, neither understand? have ye your heart yet hardened? Having eyes, see ye not? and having ears, hear ye not? How is it that ye do not understand?" (Mark 8:17-18, 21). Even in the moment of his final departure from them, their words showed that they still believed the kingdom of God was an earthly political entity and not the realm of spirit (Acts 1:6).

This being so, the Gospels themselves must be approached with grave caution and with the awareness that Jesus was not the creator of a new religion, but a messenger of the Eternal Religion he had learned in India. As a priest of the Saint Thomas Christian Church of South India once commented to me: "You cannot understand the teachings of Jesus if you do not know the scriptures of India." And if you do know the scriptures of India you can see where–however well-intentioned they may have been–the authors of the Gospels often completely missed the point and garbled the words and ideas they heard from Jesus, even attributing to him incidents from the life of Buddha and mistaking his quotations from the Upanishads, the Bhagavad Gita and the Dhammapada for doctrines original to him. For example, the opening verse of the Gospel of John: "In the beginning was the Word, and the Word was with God," which has been cited through the centuries as proof of the unique character and mission of Jesus, is really a paraphrase of the Vedic verse: "In the beginning was Prajapati, and with Him was the Word." (*Prajapati vai idam agra asit. Tasya vak dvitiya asit.* This is found in the Krishna Yajurveda, Kathaka Samhita, 12.5, 27.1; Krishna Yajurveda, Kathakapisthala Samhita, 42.1; and the Jaiminiya Brahmana II, Samaveda, 2244).

Having adopted the completely erroneous idea that Jesus was God incarnate rather than a great yoga siddha, and misunderstanding much of his teachings, things could only go downhill for them and their followers, until the true Gospel of Christ was buried beneath two millennia of confusion and theological debris. The true teachings of Jesus are to be found in their original sources, the Upanishads and the Bhagavad Gita, for he preached no new religion but the eternal truth he had learned in India.

Return to India–not ascension

It is generally supposed that at the end of his ministry in Israel Jesus ascended into heaven. But Saint Matthew and Saint John, the two Evangelists that were eye-witnesses of his departure, do not even mention such a thing, for they knew that he returned to India. Saint Mark and Saint Luke, who were not there, simply speak of Jesus being taken up into the heavens. The truth is that he departed to India, though it is not unlikely that he did rise up and "fly" there. This form of travel is not unknown to the Himalayan yogis even today.

That Jesus did not leave the world at the age of thirty-three was written about by Saint Irenaeus of Lyon in the second century. He claimed that Jesus lived to be fifty or more years old before leaving the earth, though he also said that Jesus was crucified at the age of thirty-three. This would mean that Jesus lived twenty years or more after the crucifixion. This assertion of Saint Irenaeus has puzzled Christian scholars for centuries, but if we put it together with other traditions it becomes comprehensible. Basilides of Alexandria, Mani of Persia, and Julian the Emperor said that Jesus had gone to India after His crucifixion.

Why did Jesus return to India? Anna Catharine Emmerich said that in her visions of Jesus' life she clearly saw that in India Jesus loved the people and was wholeheartedly loved in return. Even more, everyone there understood everything Jesus had to say and teach. In contrast, he was little liked in Israel and virtually no one knew what he was talking about. This would certainly be an inducement to return to India.

There may be another reason. Some contemporary anthropologists and historians believe that Jesus' ancestor Abraham was a member of the Yadava clan of Western India, the family of Krishna, who disappeared from India after Krishna's departure from this world. Swami Bhaktivedanta, founder of the Hare Krishna movement said the same. If this is so, then Jesus was really returning to the homeland of his ancestors.

And finally, Jesus may have realized that his teachings could only be preserved in land of their origin. An ancient Chinese text on the history of religions and their doctrines, known as *The Glass Mirror*, had this to say about Lord Isha (Jesus) and His teachings: "Yesu, the teacher and founder of the religion, was born miraculously.... His doctrines did not spread extensively, but *survived only in Asia*."

Some Buddhist historical records about Jesus

A contemporary written record of the life and teachings of Jesus in India was discovered in 1887 by the Russian traveler Nicholas Notovitch during his wanderings in Ladakh. He had it translated from the Tibetan text (the original, kept in the Marbour monastery near Lhasa, was in Pali) and, despite intense opposition from Christians in Russia and Europe, published it in his book *The Unknown Life of Jesus Christ*. When in Rome presenting his findings, he was advised by two high-ranking church officials that he should not print the book. One of them, however, told him that there were manuscripts dealing with Jesus' life and study in India kept in secret in the Vatican library.

As would be expected, the authenticity of Notovitch's book was attacked by the Christian missionaries and various articles written claiming that the monks of the Himis monastery, where Notovitch had found the manuscript, told investigators that they knew nothing of Notovitch or the text. But both Swami Abhedananda and Swami Trigunatitananda—direct disciples of Sri Ramakrishna and preachers of Vedanta in America—went at separate times to the Himis monastery. The monks there not only assured them that Notovitch had spent some time in the monastery as he claimed, they also showed them the manuscript, part of which they translated for Swami Abhedananda, who knew from having read Notovitch's book that it was indeed the same writing found in *The Unknown Life of Jesus Christ*. Subsequently, Abhedananda had the English translation of Notovitch's text printed in India where the Christian authorities had until then prohibited both its publication and its importation and sale. Immediately after the publication of the English edition of Notovitch's book, the British Government in India hired Moslems to go throughout Ladakh and neighboring areas posing as Hindus in search of further manuscripts about Jesus in India. They were to buy the manuscripts and bring them to their employers to be destroyed. Whether this shameful ruse succeeded to any degree we have no knowledge.

Swami Trigunatitananda not only saw the manuscript in Himis, he also was shown two paintings of Jesus. One was a depiction of his conversation with the Samaritan Woman at the well. The other was of Jesus meditating in the Himalayan forest surrounded by wild beasts that were tamed by his very presence. In America the Swami described the painting to an artist who produced the following:

(JESUS CHRIST IN HIS YOGA POSTURE.)

"HE WAS THERE IN THE WILDERNESS...
AND WAS WITH THE WILD BEASTS." S. MARK I. 13.

In 1921 the Himis monastery was visited by Henrietta Merrick who in her book *In the World's Attic* tells of learning about the records of Jesus' life that were kept there. She wrote: "In Leh is the legend of Jesus who is called Issa, and the Monastery at Himis holds precious documents fifteen hundred years old which tell of the days that he passed in Leh where he was joyously received and where he preached."

Later, in 1925, Dr. Nicholas Roerich, the renowned scholar, philosopher, and explorer, traveled in Ladakh and also was shown the manuscript and assured by the monks that Jesus had indeed lived in several Buddhist monasteries during his "lost years." According to Alexandre Andreyev's *The Myth of the Masters Revived: The Occult Lives of Nikolai and Elena Roerich*, in the original Russian version of the travelogue, Nicholas Roerich was outspoken about the authenticity of Notovitch's story and the existence of the Tibetan manuscripts. "We have learnt about the authenticity of the manuscript," Roerich is quoted as writing in Russian by Andreyev. "In Hemis indeed lies an old Tibetan translation from the manuscript, written in Pali and preserved in a well-known monastery near Lhasa. Tales about forgery are exploded." Roerich was told about the legends of Issa passed down orally. These stories were known in the region, long before the arrival of Christian missionaries.

In 1939 Elizabeth Caspari visited the Himis monastery. The Abbot showed her some scrolls, which he allowed her to examine, saying: "These books say your Jesus was here."

Robert Ravicz, a former professor of anthropology at California State University at Northridge, visited Himis in 1975. A Ladakh physician he met there spoke of Jesus' having been there during his "lost years."

In the late 1970s Edward Noack, author of *Amidst Ice and Nomads in High Asia*, and his wife visited the Himis monastery. A monk there told him: "There are manuscripts in our library that describe the journey of Jesus to the East."

Toward the end of the twentieth century the diaries of a Moravian missionary Karl Marx were discovered in which he writes of Notovitch and his finding of scrolls about "Saint Issa." Marx's diaries are kept in the Moravian Mission museum. The pages about Notovitch and the scrolls have "disappeared" and their existence is now denied in an attempt to discredit Notovitch, but before their disappearance they were photographed by a European researcher and have been made public.

Notovitch also claimed that the Vatican Library had sixty-three manuscripts from India, China, Egypt, and Arabia, all giving information about Jesus' life.

In 1812, Meer Izzut-oolah, a Persian, was sent to Ladakh and central Asia by the East India Company. Though religion was not his mission, he observed much and subsequently wrote in his book *Travels in Central Asia*: "They keep sculptured representations of departed saints, prophets and lamas in their temples for contemplation. Some of these figures are said to represent a certain prophet who is living in the heavens, which would appear to point to Jesus Christ."

When Swami Abhedananda was in the Himis monastery doing his research on the records of Jesus life in India, he was told by the abbot that Jesus had not departed from the earth at the time his apostles saw him ascend, but that he had returned to India where he lived with the Himalayan yogis for many years.

The Nathanamavali

The Bengali educator and patriot, Bipin Chandra Pal, published an autobiographical sketch in which he revealed that Vijay Krishna Goswami, a renowned saint of Bengal and a disciple of Sri Ramakrishna, told him about spending time in the Aravalli mountains with a group of extraordinary ascetic monk-yogis known as Nath Yogis. The monks spoke to him about Isha Nath, whom they looked upon as one of the great teachers of their order. When Vijay Krishna expressed interest in this venerable guru, they read out his life as recorded in one of their sacred books, the *Nathanamavali*. It was the life of him whom the Goswami knew as Jesus the Christ! Regarding the Nath Yogis' tradition, Sri Pal comments: "It is also their conjecture that Jesus Christ and this Isha Nath are one and the same person." Here is the relevant portion of the *Nathanamavali*:

"Isha Natha came to India at the age of fourteen. After this he returned to his own country and began preaching. Soon after, his brutish and materialistic countrymen conspired against him and had him crucified. After crucifixion, or perhaps even before it, Isha Natha entered samadhi by means of yoga. [Yogis often leave their bodies in samadhi, so it is not amiss to say that Jesus did indeed "die" on the cross.]

"Seeing him thus, the Jews presumed he was dead, and buried him in a tomb. At that very moment however, one of his gurus, the great Chetan Natha, happened to be in profound meditation in the lower reaches of the Himalayas, and he saw in a vision the tortures which Isha Natha was undergoing. He therefore made his body lighter than air and passed over to the land of Israel.

"The day of his arrival was marked with thunder and lightning, for the gods were angry with the Jews, and the whole world trembled. When Chetan Natha arrived, he took the body of Isha Natha from the tomb, woke him from his samadhi, and later led him off to the sacred land of the Aryans. Isha Natha then established an ashram in the lower regions of the Himalayas and he established the cult of the lingam there." ("The cult of the lingam" refers to the Shaivite branch of Hinduism. We will speak more on that later.)

This assertion is supported by two relics of Jesus which are presently found in Kashmir. One is his staff, which is kept in the monastery of Aish-Muqan and is made accessible to the public in times of public catastrophe such as floods or epidemics.

The other is the Stone of Moses—a Shiva linga that had belonged to

Moses and which Jesus brought to Kashmir. This linga is kept in the Shiva temple at Bijbehara in Kashmir. One hundred and eight pounds

in weight, if eleven people put one finger on the stone and recite the bija mantra "Ka" over and over, it will rise three feet or so into the air and remain suspended as long as the recitation continues. "Shiva" means one who is auspicious and gives blessings and happiness. In ancient Sanskrit the word *ka* means to please and to satisfy–that which Shiva does for His worshippers.

I have met two people who have "raised the Stone of Moses." One of them said that the number required to raise the stone relates to their spiritual development, and that he had raised it with only three others.

The Bhavishya Maha Purana

One ancient book of Kashmiri history, the *Bhavishya Maha Purana*, gives the following account of the meeting of a king of Kashmir with Jesus sometime after the middle of the first century:

"When the king of the Sakas came to the Himalayas, he saw a dignified person of golden complexion wearing a long white robe. Astonished to see this foreigner, he asked, 'Who are you?' The dignified person replied in a pleasant manner: 'Know me as Son of God [Isha Putram], or Born of a Virgin [Kumarigarbhasang-bhawam]. Being given to truth and penances, I preached the Dharma to the mlecchas.... O King, I hail from a land far away, where there is no truth, and evil knows no limits. I appeared in the country of the mlecchas [barbarians] as Isha Masiha [Jesus Messiah/Christ] and I suffered at their hands. For I said unto them, "'Remove all mental and bodily impurities. Remember the Name of our Lord God. Meditate upon Him Whose abode is in the center of the sun.'" There in the land of mleccha darkness, I taught love, truth, and purity of heart. I asked human beings to serve the Lord. But I suffered at the hands of the wicked and the guilty. In truth, O King, all power rests with the Lord, Who is in the center of the sun. And the elements, and the cosmos, and the sun, and God Himself, are forever. Perfect, pure, and blissful,

God is always in my heart. Thus my Name has been established as Isha Masiha.' After having heard the pious words from the lips of this distinguished person, the king felt peaceful, made obeisance to him, and returned" (*Bhavishya Maha Purana* 3.2.9-31. The word *mleccha* means a foreigner, a non-Indian.)

Another Kashmiri history, the *Rajatarangini*, written in 1148 A.D., says that a great saint named Issana lived at Issabar on the bank of Dal Lake and had many disciples, one of which he raised from the dead. (Would this be Lazarus?)

When teaching in Israel, Jesus told the people: "Other sheep I have, which are not of this fold" (John 10:16), speaking of his Eastern disciples. For when Jesus came to the Jordan at the beginning of his ministry, he had spent more years of his life in India than in Israel. And he returned there for the remainder of his life, because he was a spiritual son of India: the Christ of India, messenger of Sanatana Dharma to the West.

Swami Sivananda

As Swami Sivananda of Rishikesh wrote in *Lives of Saints*:

"[Lord Jesus] disappeared at the ages of thirteen and reappeared in his thirty-first year. During this period, from his thirteenth to his thirty-first year, he came to India and practiced Yoga....Jesus left Jerusalem and reached the land of Indus in the company of merchants. He visited Varanasi, Rajgriha and other places in India. He spent several years in Hindustan. Jesus lived like a Hindu or a Buddhist monk, a life of burning renunciation and dispassion. He assimilated the ideals, precepts and principles of Hinduism. *Christianity is modified Hinduism only*, which was suitable for those people who lived in the period of Christ. Really speaking, Jesus was a child of the soil of India only. That is the reason why there is so much of similarity between his teachings and the teachings of Hinduism and Buddhism. During [this period] he travelled in India where he got initiation from sages and seers."

And in his essay simply titled "Christianity" he also wrote:

"Christian faith sprung from the wisdom of India overspread the old trunk of Judaism. Buddhism prevailed in Palestine when Christ was born. Christ himself came in contact with it through John the Baptist. There is a striking resemblance between Buddhism and Christianity in their precepts, in their forms and ceremonies, in the architectural style of their temples, and even in the account of the lives of their founders.

"...Christianity owes to Buddhism that higher morality which distinguishes it from Judaism. The moral precepts and teachings of Buddhism have much in common with those of Christianity.

"Between his thirteenth and thirty-second years of age, Jesus spent his life in India and lived like a Hindu or Buddhist monk. He had burning Vairagya (dispassion) and spirit of renunciation. In India he assimilated Hindu ideals and principles.

"His words have been misunderstood, wrongly annotated, mutilated, deformed and transformed and yet they have survived almost two thousand years as they were very powerful and came from the heart of a realized Yogi.

"Here is the gist of Jesus' teachings: God is Spirit. He is omnipresent. He loves His creatures with infinite love. He is the Father of all. God is immanent in the world. He is transcendental also. He sent His son Jesus Christ unto the world to show them the way to attain immortality."

Satya Sai Baba

In a public talk printed in January of 1978 in *Sanatana Sarati*, Sri Satya Sai Baba spoke of Jesus' spiritual aspirations in Israel, and said:

"Here [in India], his stay in the Himalayan monasteries, in Kashmir and other centres of eastern asceticism and philosophical enquiry brought him greater success. From the attitude of being a messenger of God, he declared that he was the Son of God, after

returning from the East." He also stated: "In the Tibetan manuscript at the monastery where Isha spent some years the name is
written as Issa. The name Isha means 'the Lord of all living beings.'
Jesus proclaimed that he was a messenger of God, he wanted to
emphasize that everyone is a messenger of God and has to speak,
act and think as one. This is the true *karma kanda* of the Vedas,
the spiritual discipline of work, of repetition of the name of the
Lord, of meditation, of service."

The doubting of the Apostle Thomas

THE APOSTLE OF INDIA

Master and disciple

In India it is often said that "the father is born again in the son." This ancient adage applies also to the worthy disciple—in him the master continues his work. This being so, the character and mission of Jesus the Christ of India can be traced in that of his apostle Thomas. Thomas is a nickname derived from the Syrian (Aramaic) word *t'omo*, which means "twin." The apostle's true name was Judas, as is recorded in the ancient Syriac gospel texts, but it was not used in later gospel texts so he would neither bear the name of the Betrayer nor be mistakenly identified with him by those who would read or hear them read.

Saint Thomas the Apostle in India

After the departure of Jesus from Israel, when the other apostles began going through the Mediterranean world and preaching, Judas Thomas, the Twin, did not. His assignment had been given him by Jesus himself. Thomas was to depart for India where he would live in the Himalayas with Jesus and those great masters who had taught Jesus before him. This was because Jesus had destined him to become the spiritual twin of his master, the most true in his likeness to Jesus both inwardly and outwardly.

(It is a matter of record that Judas Thomas was also physically identical to Jesus. This was unusual but not impossible or even unknown, since he was a cousin of Jesus, as were most of the apostles.)

So overwhelming did this task seem to Saint Thomas that he tried to avoid his mission. Yet it was not long before a government official from India came to Israel to find an architect for his king, who wished a palace built by an artisan from the land of the renowned Hiram Abiff, whose construction of the temple of Solomon was known throughout the world. Jesus manifested to him in a physical body and sold Saint Thomas to the man as a slave, giving him a signed document to that effect. When confronted with this document, Saint Thomas abandoned his resistance and left for India where he did in truth follow the steps of his master and become his twin in all things.

In the life of Saint Thomas written by the Christian Gnostic Bardaisan (154-222), based on letters written by Saint Thomas, perhaps to his Persian disciples, he is referred to as: "Twin brother of Christ, apostle of the Highest who shares in the knowledge of the hidden word of Christ, recipient of his secret pronouncements." Regarding the records of Jesus' life that he found in the Himis monastery, Nicholoas Notovitch wrote this interesting remark in relation to Saint Thomas: "[The scrolls] may have actually been spoken by St. Thomas, historical sketches having been traced by his own hand or under his direction."

Return to the West

In the Himalayas Saint Thomas was reunited with Jesus until he received the inner call to return to the West for the impending departure of the Virgin Mary from this earthly life. Just as he had been separated from his brother apostles for a special mission, so he was in the final hour of the Virgin's life. For he did not reach Ephesus in time to be present at her going forth from the body, but only came there on foot the third day after her burial. As he was approaching her tomb unawares, he was astounded to see her radiant living body emerge from the stone sepulcher and ascend. Realizing that she had finished her span of life without his being present, and fearing that he would never see her divine form again, he cried out to her in anguish of heart, imploring her not to leave him desolate. Looking upon him with loving tenderness, the Virgin took from her waist the belt she habitually wore and threw it down to him with words of blessing.

Carrying the precious relic of her belt, Saint Thomas hastened into Ephesus and announced to the grieving apostles and all those gathered in the Mother's house that she, too, was risen from the dead. Whereas he had doubted the good news of Jesus' resurrection and had received proof of its reality by touching the resurrected body of his Lord, now it was Thomas who gave physical evidence that Mary, too, was "alive for evermore" (Revelation 1:18). Saint Thomas took the Virgin Mother's belt with him to India, and there it became the most valued treasure of his disciples.

To Qumran and India

Before returning to south India for the fulfillment of his commission from Jesus, Saint Thomas went to visit the Essene communities of Israel, urging that some of them come with him to India to both escape the imminent destruction by the Romans and to help him in his spiritual work. Many did so, and a company of Essenes headed by Saint Thomas arrived in South India (Kerala) in 52 A.D. These Essenes started several villages in the same area. At the end of the twentieth century those sites were excavated and many coins like those found in the Qumran caves were unearthed.

A Hindu Brahmin family near the town of Palur, Kerala, has a document of family history wherein it is written: "In the Kali year 3153 [52 A.D.] the foreigner Thomas [Toma] Sannyasi came to our village and preached there." It is noteworthy that Saint Thomas is described as a Hindu monk (sannyasi), which he would have to have been if he truly followed in the steps of Jesus.

Ancient records say that frequently Jesus was seen in South India and mistaken for Saint Thomas. He and Saint Thomas were sometimes seen speaking together, and it could not be known which was which. Apparently Jesus occasionally came down from his Himalayan abode to visit Saint Thomas and supervise his work.

The disciples of Saint Thomas

In Mylapore near modern Madras, the apostle Thomas was pierced with a lance on December 19, 72 A.D., but did not die until December 21. He was buried nearby, and the earth from his tomb worked many miracles. In 1292 Marco Polo visited his tomb and took some of the red-colored earth from there. Upon his return to Venice he healed many people with it according to his own testimony.

Since in India Jesus was known as "Isha" (the Lord), the disciples of Saint Thomas preferred to be called Ishannis, "of Isha" (just as Lutheran means "of Luther"). Nearly all those who accepted the teachings of Saint Thomas were devout Brahmins of the highest level (Nambudiri and Nair—many of them who had emigrated from Kashmir to Kerala) who were Shaivites of the strictest order. So strict and correct were the disciples of Saint Thomas in their Brahminical character and observance that they were frequently asked by the other Hindus to perform the rites of purification (*shuddhi karanam*) for defiled objects and even of Hindu temples. Thus the disciples of Saint Thomas were mostly of the Brahmin caste.

Naassenes

Ancient Indian historical records sometimes refer to the disciples of Saint Thomas as Naassenes. This may be a corruption of "Essene" but in the ancient Gnostic Christian texts discovered at Nag Hammadi, Egypt, we find the term "Nazoreans," so the Ishannis may also have used it in referring to themselves. If so, this would indicate their esoteric character and affinity with the Gnostics of Egypt—most of whom were Essenes or descendants of Essenes. Regarding the Essenes, Alfred Edersheim, in his nineteenth century classic *The Life and Times of Jesus the Messiah*, wrote: "The general movement had passed beyond the bounds of Judaism, and appeared in some forms of the Gnostic heresy."

Because of the great number of Saint Thomas' disciples, Jewish and Indian, in the southernmost state of Kerala, it is sometimes called "the country of the Nazaranis" even today. The daily train from Madras to Kerala is known as "the Nazarani Express."

Tamil historical records contemporaneous with Saint Thomas say that he taught "a Buddhist religion." This was no doubt because of Saint Thomas' intense monastic and philosophic nature which contrasted with the usual form of Hinduism at that time, which consisted mostly of external rituals and the use of religion to attain utterly materialistic goals (*karma khanda*). In the same way, such Hindus often called Adi Shankaracharya and his followers Buddhists, as some extreme Vaishnavas do even today.

Surya Vamsa

For centuries among the other Hindus in referring to them, the Ishannis were also called Surya Vamsa, and this term was even used on occasion in major legal documents. Surya Vamsa means "People of the Sun," Surya being a Sanskrit word for the sun. This is only logical if we remember the words of Jesus to the king of Kashmir: "I said unto them, 'Remove all mental and bodily impurities. Remember the Name of our Lord God. Meditate upon Him Whose abode is in the center of the sun.'... In truth, O King, all power rests with the Lord, Who is in the center of the sun."

The Ishanni Sampradaya

A sampradaya is a lineage of spiritual teaching stemming from an enlightened teacher, such as the Shankara Sampradaya, Ramanuja Sampradaya, Madhavacharya Sampradaya, or according to the form of God they particularly worship such as the Shaivite, Vaishnava, Shakta, or Ganapatya sampradayas. Whatever distinctive customs a sampradaya might possess, they all consider themselves to be fundamentally followers of Sanatana Dharma, the religion based on the Vedas and the teachings of the vedic seers known as rishis. And the majority of their customs and spiritual doctrines are absolutely identical and harmonious with one another.

The disciples of Saint Thomas were considered a sampradaya within Sanatana Dharma, not a separate religion. It is historical fact that they were an integral part of Hindu society in every way.

Bar-Hebraeus, an early Syrian Christian writer, records that when Christians from Persia visited India the Saint Thomas Christians told them: "We are the disciples of Saint Thomas." It was those Persians who created the phrase "Saint Thomas Christians" and first began to use it. But it was not used by the descendants of the first disciples of Saint Thomas. This fact underscores their fundamental difference from the religion derived from the other apostles.

The witness of history

History itself demonstrates the character of the disciples of Saint Thomas as a Shaivite sampradaya within Hindu religion.

In 345 A.D., when the ruler of Carnellur gave the suburb of Muziris to the Ishannis for their exclusive use, they renamed it Mahadevar Pattanam, the City of Mahadeva (Shiva). The king, a Hindu, laid the first brick for the Ishanni temple that was built there, and upon its completion he led the first service of prayers to be conducted there. This would not have been done if the Ishannis were not themselves considered part of Hinduism. Eventually an Ishanni kingdom (district), with Mahadevar Pattanam as its capital, was established.

Whenever a child reached the age of three years the Ishannis always had a Brahmin pandit come to their home and symbolically begin his formal education by guiding the child's fingers to trace the mantra *Om*

Sri Ganapataye Namah–"I bow to Lord Ganesha"–in a plate of rice before which a ghee lamp was burning that had previously been worshipped as an emblem of the goddess Saraswati, the goddess of wisdom and learning. Ganesha is the Hindu deity that is depicted with the head of an elephant and is the son of Shiva. He is always worshipped before any undertaking, including, in this instance, the beginning of education.

It is interesting that many of the very old Ishanni (now Saint Thomas Christian) temples in South India have golden "dharma towers" in front of them just like those in the temples of Vishnu.

The beginning of the end

Because Kerala was a center of international trade, some contact took place between the Ishannis and the Christians of the Middle East and Europe. Some of these reported in the fourth century that the Ishannis had "lost their priesthood," not understanding that Jesus and Saint Thomas were Nath Yogis who considered Sanatana Dharma and Yoga to be sufficient and had not taught or practiced anything else. After some centuries the Syrian Christians, some of which settled in Kerala, persuaded the Ishannis to adopt their rituals and worship. Nevertheless their distinctive ways and identity were preserved.

At the coming of the Portuguese colonialists to India in large numbers, however, this began to change. Christians from Europe were always received in total friendship by the Ishannis and often given places to live. In many instances the Ishannis interceded with the local rulers in gaining residency and trade permissions for the Europeans. But sadly, on the part of the opportunistic Europeans there was no such sincere openness, and as soon as any political ascendancy was attained, pressure was brought to bear on the Ishannis to convert to the Christianity of the Westerners.

This came to an appalling climax in the last year of the sixteenth century when the Portuguese Roman Catholic Archbishop of Goa, Alexius Menezes, summoned all the Ishanni clergy and a considerable number

of laymen to the town of Diamper to supposedly bring peace and rec-
onciliation between them and the Portuguese Catholics. In response
one hundred fifty-three priests and about six hundred and sixty laymen
attended. The Ishannis were asked to bring all their liturgical and theological texts–especially their ancient texts containing the teachings of
Saint Thomas–so they could be "examined." Believing that the Europeans
wanted to sincerely discover the spiritual traditions of Saint Thomas,
and therefore of Jesus, they did so. Their horror was boundless when
they found themselves surrounded by Portuguese soldiers who forced
them at gunpoint to surrender their precious manuscripts, which were
then burned in their presence at the order of the Archbishop. Because
of this "It is not possible to write a complete history of the Christians
in South-West India, because the ancient documents of their churches
were destroyed by fire at the Synod of Diamper in 1599," as Cardinal
Tisserant admits.

"What history will not willingly forgive is the literary holocaust which
was carried out on the authority of this decree, when all books that could
be laid hands on were consigned to the flames. It was comparable in
many ways with the vandalism of Omar, who by similar wanton destruction ordered the noble library of Alexandria to be consumed by flames.
The Syrian Christians of today believe that because of this cruel decree,
no records are available with them to recover and establish beyond all
dispute their past Church history. None will deny that there is some
substance in this belief" (S. G. Pothen, *The Syrian Christians of Kerala*).

Among the books burned were many copies of three books. Two of
them, *The Book of Charms* and *The Ring of Solomon*, were books of Christian magic. The third was a book on esoteric healing and the making of
amulets from gems and herbs (as the Essenes had also done) called *The
Medicine of the Persians*. They now exist only as nearly-forgotten names.

Not only were the books brought to Diamper destroyed, Archbishop
Menezes later went from church to church searching for more books
and burning entire libraries in many places–even in areas where the

Portuguese had no political jurisdictions whatsoever. The liturgical texts containing the rites of the Saint Thomas Christians were especially sought out and destroyed because they revealed how utterly the other churches had departed from the original ways of Christianity, and because they expressed the correct view of Jesus as a Son of God by attainment and not as the creator God incarnate. A list of forbidden books was made at Diamper, and any who read or listened to them being read were automatically condemned.

Over the course of the next days the Archbishop also engaged in harangues to "correct" the ways of the Ishannis (henceforth to be known as "Saint Thomas Christians") and bring them into conformity with those of "the one, holy, catholic, and apostolic See of Rome."

The official acts of the Synod particularly inveighed against the Ishannis who taught school and made provisions for the religious instructions of the students in Hindu religion, keeping the images of Hindu deities in the schools so the students could learn and perform their daily worship. Those who sent their children to schools taught by Hindus where they, too, worshipped the deities, were declared excommunicated (from a church to which they did not even belong!) and the children were forbidden to enter anything but a Portuguese-established church.

The Ishanni participation in the worship of Hindu temples was the norm for them since they were a Hindu sampradaya, so that, too, was soundly castigated. Especially denounced was the use of Hindu rites of exorcism by the Ishanni priests, as well as other "idolatrous" and "superstitious" Vedic rituals. Priests who dared to have themselves registered as Nair Brahmins were condemned, not for a religious reason, but because it supposedly made them liable to be called up for military service.

Saint Thomas had given the Ishannis a book which they used for divination to obtain guidance in the making of important decisions and to determine the future. This was a special target of the Portuguese, who also railed against their practice of divination, and all copies of this invaluable document were consigned to the flames of bigotry.

The Ishannis considered astrology a legitimate means of forecast and guidance, and used it accordingly. Their priests were considered to be especially skilled in determining astrologically what days and times were the most favorable for marriage and the starting of journeys or any other type of endeavor. This is still retained by the Saint Thomas Christians in Kerala. In David Daniel's book *The Orthodox Church of India*, published and sold by the Orthodox Church in India, we find this: "The Saint Thomas Christians are accustomed to consult astrologers to ascertain the auspicious moment for setting out for any purpose, e.g., for a journey, a wedding, etc. Drawing horoscopes is not uncommon amongst them." Many of the Saint Thomas Christian priests to this day are astrologers and considered specialists in determining fortunate or auspicious times.

Oddly, condemnation was even pronounced against the Ishannis' laudable custom of adopting as many orphans as they could so they would not be homeless. This was a custom they had inherited from the Essenes.

They were also condemned for piercing their ears and taking too many baths in a day! Being Brahmins, this was perfectly normal for them.

The Synod of Diamper did have one positive effect, though a backhanded one. By reading the fulminations against the "pagan" ways of the Ishannis and the official condemnations of them we are able to establish that the they were indeed orthodox Hindu Brahmins who revered Jesus as a teacher but considered themselves one with the other segments (sampradayas) of Hinduism.

The aftermath

Hardly any of the Ishannis could even understand the language in which all this was done, and they were forced through cajolery and threats to sign documents of concurrence with all that had taken place–these documents being represented to them as nothing more than statements that they had been present at the gathering. Before sending those documents to Rome, Archbishop Menezes interpolated many items into the signed documents to make it appear that they had agreed to things either not actually spoken about or that were firmly resisted by them when they were brought up.

Finally, "approved" Syriac (Aramaic) liturgical texts were issued to the clergy along with other written directives, and they departed in a daze to their flocks, accompanied by Portuguese "assistants" who were to make sure that they carried out the demands of the Europeans.

When the Jesuits that were present at the Diamper assembly officially objected to the outrageous actions of Archbishop Menezes, he coolly remarked that "he behaved like that just to show the way of salvation to the assembled without hindrance." Cardinal Eugene Tisserant was apparently of the same mentality when, in 1957, he wrote in *Eastern Christianity in India*: "Instead of destroying the existing Syriac manuscripts, he [Archbishop Menezes] could have had them corrected, but his method was that of certainty, so that any future heresy could be more easily averted."

Thus was the beginning of the great loss of identity and knowledge which today is no doubt irreparable. Some were the results of persecution and some the results of false friendship and influence on the part of Western missionaries. In this way both Catholic and Protestant Europe managed to wreak undeniable and profound damage on the Saint Thomas Christian Church. Slowly the Ishanni (Hindu) traditions were eroded until today only tokens remain. Their subsequent history and identity is so confused that even the Saint Thomas Christians of today are not sure about much of it. I have met Saint Thomas Christians that were basically standard contemporary Eastern Orthodox Christians, some that were more like rabid Protestant fundamentalists, and some that identified with Hinduism, kept the pictures and images of the deities, wore the sacred thread and rudraksha beads and put Shaivite marks on their forehead, and actively campaigned to wipe out all the innovations of the intervening centuries and return to their status as a Hindu sampradaya with traditional temples and worship.

I saw the effects of this for myself when speaking at a church meeting in Niranam where Saint Thomas had founded the congregation. (Several examples of his woodwork–especially carvings in traditional Hindu temple style, since all the Ishanni temples were in that style–were shown to me.) During my talk, I felt so galled by not being able to speak freely of the higher, esoteric aspects of religion that I decided to break loose and say what I pleased, and hang the consequences. At the far back many very elderly men and women had been sitting with their heads bowed down in abject boredom and disinterest. But when I had spoken just a few sentences of real Christian belief, they all began looking eagerly at me, smiling, nodding and gesturing to one another in approval. At the end they all surged forward to express their appreciation of my talk. It was evident that as children they had heard the very things I was now speaking, but it had been a long and dreary time since those truths had been publicly expressed

Saint Gregorios of Parumala

The crowning glory of Saint Thomas Christianity was the great bishop-saint Gregorios of Parumala, who lived in the nineteenth century. Every day in the major newspapers of Kerala strings of identical small icons of Saint Gregorios are printed, each one a thanksgiving for an answered prayer. In one city of Kerala I saw a shrine to Saint Gregorios at a bus stop with hundreds of candles burning before his icon in petition for those who had prayed there before proceeding on to work or school. The money contributed for the candles was there in an open box, but no one would think of stealing from it. It is a common sight along the roads in Kerala to see large wayside shrines with more-than-life-size icons of the saint enshrined in them.

The tomb of Saint Gregorios in Parumala is visited daily by thousands and tens of thousands of pilgrims–Hindus, Christians, and Moslems–for whom it flows miracles and blessings beyond counting. I can bear witness that the moment you enter the boundaries of the island-shrine

Saint Gregorios of Parumala (1848-1902)

you step into another world altogether, and that the room where he left his body is one of the most spiritually powerful places I have ever been. Fortunately I was able to meditate there for some time.

Here in America I met a remarkable yogi and Hindu scholar, Sri Nandu Menon. He told me that Saint Gregorios was the best friend of his strictly traditional Hindu Brahmin uncles, and spent a great deal of time with them in spiritual discussions. Nanduji told me that Saint Gregorios told his uncles that he considered his mission in life was to bring about the restoration of three essential teachings to the Saint Thomas Christian Church: 1) the belief in karma; 2) the belief in reincarnation; and 3) the belief that God and the individual spirit-self are one. Unfortunately it did not come about in India to the degree he desired.

The situation today

Despite the sad picture I have just given of the Saint Thomas Christian Church having lost most of its heritage from Saint Thomas, the good news is that history itself shows that Jesus was a Sanatana Dharmi and a Nath Yogi. And both traditions are intact and flourishing today. Therefore those who wish to truly be "of Christ" and follow him need only ensure that they are genuine adherents of Sanatana Dharma and Yoga. I say this because many sincere Westerners really do not know authentic dharma or yoga since they have believed those who themselves are neither dharmis or yogis—especially the "gurus" that abound in the West and throughout the world. The purpose of our website, ocoy.org, is to assist them in finding their way to real dharma and yoga.

After the Roman Catholic Portuguese authorities had assassinated Mar Ahatalla, a Syriac Orthodox bishop who had come to India to find out why the Saint Thomas Christian Church had lapsed in its contacts with the Syriac Patriarchate, a multitude of Saint Thomas Christians gathered at Saint Mary's Church at Mattancherry on January 3, 1653 and took a solemn oath on the Coonan Cross to no longer have any connection whatsoever with the Roman Church.

So many had come for this oath-taking, that ropes were tied to the cross and the oath-takers held on to the ropes in order to be "touching" the cross. After this oath was taken, 199,600 Saint Thomas Christians severed all relations with the Roman Church, only 400 remaining loyal to Rome. Since that time the Saint Thomas Church has remained autonomous, its chief bishop bearing the title of Catholicos, as do some other heads of Eastern Churches such as the Armenian Apostolic Church, the Assyrian Church of the East and the Georgian Orthodox Church.

The most important part of this picture is the clothing and hair of all the Saint Thomas Christians depicted taking the oath. They are wearing the Brahminical sacred thread, a sign of orthodox Hindu religion, as well as the shikha at the back top of the head, another symbol of the Brahmin caste.

The Saint Thomas Christian Cross

The Beliefs of Original Christianity

"All the religions of the world have come into existence through the will of God, and all will cease to exist through His will. But the religion of India will never cease to exist, for it alone is the Sanatana [Eternal] Dharma." Sri Ramakrishna Paramhansa

Considering the foregoing pages, it is obvious that an outline of original Christian belief will be nothing more or less than a statement of classical, traditional Sanatana Dharma based on the eleven authentic Upanishads, the Bhagavad Gita, the Yoga Darshana (Yoga Sutras) and the philosophical writings of such great philosophers as Adi Shankaracharya, re-former of the ancient Swami Order.

The nature of dharma

First of all: What is dharma? Mere philosophy or theology is totally useless if it is not supported by a way of life that enables the individual to unfold and bring to perfection the qualities that are the eternal nature of every individual spirit or jiva. Those principles and practices which comprise such an enabling life are what we mean by dharma. A philosophical view is only a darshan, an intellectual view of the way things are. Such is necessary, but only insofar as it leads to the mode of living that is dharma.

True dharma was directly perceived by the rishis of India. Known as Sanatana (Eternal) Dharma, it reveals the Eternal Being, the Sanatana Purusha. That which is in accord with Sanatana Dharma is true; that which is not is untrue, because Sanatana Dharma is not a religion: it is Truth. Religions are usually degenerations of truth and confuse the issue.

In India Sanatana Dharma and Hinduism are naturally considered synonymous, though certain sects are not fully in accord with Sanatana Dharma. For example: those who believe in everlasting damnation, such as the Madhavacharya Sampradaya; those who decry and denounce as either false or inferior all forms of deity other than their particular chosen form, such as certain sectarian Shaivites, Shaktas, and Vaishnavas, and those that decry and denounce everyone and everything but themselves, such as the Radhaswami or Sant Mat sects. Many of today's Hindu Fundamentalists are much more akin to Moslem and Christian Fundamentalists than to real Hindus.

Dharma is eternal

The principles of dharma, like the principles of mathematics, are both eternal and universal in their application. Just as mathematics has no originator or author or connotation of any culture, the same is true of dharma. Dharma is discovered, not created, by human beings. For example, "Euclidian Geometry" was discovered by the Greek Euclid, but it is not Greek in any way and carries no connotation of Hellenism.

Nevertheless, it cannot be responsibly denied that Sanatana Dharma, Eternal Truth or Religion, has been completely and perfectly imparted to us by the enlightened sages or rishis (seers) of India, many of whom are completely unknown to us by name. Their vision has been conveyed to us in various sacred texts, using Sanskrit as the perfect, exact and necessary vehicle for its expression. The essential texts for those interested in truly comprehending Sanatana Dharma are the eleven major Upanishads: Isha, Kena, Katha, Prashna, Mundaka, Mandukya, Taittiriya, Aitareya, Chandogya, Brihadaranyaka, and Shvetashvatara Upanishads, the Bhagavad Gita and the Yoga Sutras (Yoga Darshana) of Patanjali. In addition there are numberless texts that transmit Sanatana Dharma to the seeker. These include the writings of great philosophers and yogis, ancient and modern. But the ones just listed are of unquestioned reliability and authority

Dharma is universal

Wherever in the world we find any truth, philosophical or spiritual, it is a reflection of Sanatana Dharma, and is often evidence of a long-forgotten historical presence of India's influence in that part of the world. At the root of every valid religion we will find Sanatana Dharma—not just abstractly but as the historical presence just mentioned. For example, both Buddha and Jesus were nourished in the bosom of Sanatana Dharma. Those who consider themselves their followers may have strayed far from the principles which produced and empowered those two great teachers, but that in no way dims the value of Buddha and Jesus (Isha Nath) as adherents of the Eternal Dharma. Those who would follow them must of necessity look to the same fountainhead of wisdom from which they drank and came to live—and honestly and openly acknowledge it.

Dharma is not dogma

Before any exposition, it should be made very clear that the teachings of Sanatana Dharma (and therefore of original Christianity) are not a set of imposed dogmas, but rather a way of spiritual life. This is why Saint Paul, contrasting the Christian way with that of the Mosaic Law, wrote that God "hath made us able ministers of the new testament; not of the letter, but of the spirit: for the letter killeth, but the spirit giveth life" (II Corinthians 3:6). Emphasis is on spiritual practice (yoga meditation) and observance (the disciplines of yama and niyama, defined in the Glossary at the end of this book) and the experience and knowledge gained from such practice and observance, rather than the intellectual concepts of theology and dogma. There is a broad framework within which spiritual life is pursued, but theological details are left up to the individual. Yet there are certain concepts which, when rightly understood as metaphysical rules of the spiritual road, facilitate the individual's seeking. They need not be blindly believed, but it helps to accept them provisionally—that is, with an open mind and the understanding that in time the seeker will come to know for himself their truth and relevance.

The three eternals

There are three eternal things: God, the individual spirits living within the greater Being of God, and the Creative Power that manifests as the relative existence within which the spirits evolve.

Satchidananda

Satchidananda (God) is infinite, omnipresent, omniscient, and omnipotent; beginningless and endless; trinity and unity. Totally outside all things and yet within all things simultaneously. Satchidananda is Itself threefold: 1) Transcendent Existence (Brahman), 2) Consciousness Within All That Exists (Ishwara) and 3) Creative Energy (Mahashakti, Mulaprakriti), or Relative Existence, in which Ishwara is embodied and in which all the individual spirits (jivas) are evolving.

To enable those in the Mediterranean world to understand Satchidananda, Jesus spoke of Father, Son and Holy Spirit. (The word "Trinity" did not exist until two hundred years after his lifetime.) The Father is Brahman, the Son is Ishwara and the Holy Spirit (Holy Breath) is Mahashakti. It is very simple. But the word "Satchidananda" cannot be improved upon.

In some Indian texts Ishwara is spoken of as the Mahat Tattwa, the Great Principle, which means that Ishwara is the emanation-reflection of Brahman within creation, or in the mirror of creation which is the primordial matter, Mulaprakriti or Mahashakti.

It will be good to go into all this in more detail to make sure we understand all this.

Brahman

Brahman (God), is Absolute Being outside of which there can be nothing, the ever-existent Spirit, the Absolute Consciousness That encompasses all things but is encompassed by none. Therefore God is totally beyond the reach of the human intellect and utterly indefinable or intellectually comprehensible. We can easily say what God is *not*—for anything we might say will not express God—but we cannot say a single word about what God *is*.

Brahman is transcendent and beyond any qualities or conditionings whatsoever. However, with the inconsistency that is a marked trait of Eastern thinking, the ancient seers have given us a definition that enables us to get as much of a grasp of Brahman as is possible for our minds: Sat-Chit-Ananda as just discussed. However, it is more appropriate to refer to Brahman as It than as He.

Sat

Brahman does not exist in the sense that things in relativity exist. Rather, It is Existence itself. Or, more to the point, Brahman is the very ground, the basis, of existence, in and through which all things exist. Brahman is the ocean and all else are the waves. "It shining, all things shine," says the Veda, and: "Its shadow is immortality." Brahman can equally fittingly be called Reality.

Chit

Brahman is Pure Consciousness, the very Principle of Consciousness itself. It is therefore omniscient—not in the sense of just knowing all things in the present moment, but in the sense of knowing all things whatsoever—past, present, and future—simultaneously. This is because Brahman is outside of time and all things are present to It; nothing is past and nothing is future. Brahman *is* the Eternal Now. Since all things are known to him, we can say that God is conscious, as well.

Ananda

"Brahman is ever-new joy." This was the definition of Brahman given by the great Master, Paramhansa Yogananda. Brahman is not joyful, It is joy itself. Brahman, then, is ever-existent, infinitely-conscious bliss.

Primordial Energy–Mulaprakriti or Mahashakti

God as consciousness is the eternal witness, but he is also the eternal actor or creator. And this he accomplishes through his kriya shakti (power of action) known as Prakriti, the primordial power or energy. This boundless field of vibrating energy is like an ocean which manifests in many waves. Whatever exists is made up of the endless variations of this primal energy. All that can be objectively experienced (and much that seems to be internally experienced, but is actually subtle objectivity) is formed of this divine energy. For Prakriti is not an unconscious or inert substance like a cosmic clay which God sculpts, but is God himself in the form of light: divine radiance.

We can think of it in this way: Brahman by his very nature emits light, the Brahmajyoti, and this radiance ever streams forth from It eternally and boundlessly. And this Light is itself conscious, for it is Brahman. The word Brahman comes from the root *brih*, which means "to expand," so this very idea is implied in Vedic religion.

All relative existence is essentially absolute existence, and as such is the divine reality in manifestation without any loss or alternation of its nature. Thus there is no such thing as creation from nothing.

Duality in the Oneness of Brahman

Brahman (especially as Ishwara) is sometimes spoken of as "the Cosmic Egg" in the sense that It is the seed or germ of all life.

Specifically, Brahman is called Hiranyagarbha, the Golden Egg, for It shines, sending forth the radiance (tejas) that is the Great Energy, Mahashakti. And this energy is not an agent or instrument of Brahman, but *is* Brahman. Thus Brahman is both absolutely one and absolutely two. This state of things is referred to in a mantra from the upanishads that is recited daily:

> *Purnamidah, purnamidam,*
> *purnat purnamudachyate;*
> *Purnasya purnamadaya,*
> *purnam ewawashishyate.*

Purna means "total, full, complete," which is what our English term "perfect" used to mean, rather than just "without fault." In this verse, the word "complete" (purna) refers to Brahman. Here, as best I can, is a translation into English:

> This is the Complete; That is the Complete.
> The Complete has come out of the Complete.
> If we take the Complete away from the Complete,
> Only the Complete remains.

Let us say it another way: the Absolute is the Totality; the Relative is the Totality. The Relative has emanated from the Absolute. Yet if we take away either of these and consider only the one or the other, we will find that each is the Totality; even more, we will discover that the Absolute is the Relative, and the Relative is the Absolute.

It may tend to make our heads spin, but we have to realize that the unity and the duality are equally true, and that to ascribe either unity or duality to Brahman exclusive of the other is to be mistaken. To reject one is to reject the other, to accept one is to accept the other. For they are truly one.

Another point brought out by this is the impossibility of any actual conflict between the views of Brahman as personal or impersonal, immanent or transcendent. The person who knows the impersonal knows that also is the personal. And those who know the personal, know that he/she are also the impersonal.

Om Tat Sat

Om Tat Sat is a mantric formula usually spoken at the end of some act as a dedication of that act to God. It, too, refers to Satchidananda, but in a different order. Om is the indicator of cosmic vibration itself and so refers to the vibratory divine life that is Mahashakti. Tat–which means "that"–refers to Ishwara whom we can speak of and even perceive as an object. Sat is "the real" (or "the true") that is existence itself, and consequently refers to the highest, transcendent aspect of Brahman, sometimes called Parabrahman.

The individual souls (jivas)

You and I as individual consciousnesses, spirit-selves or atmas, are part of the second eternal. We are gods, exact images of Satchidananda, also consisting of three aspects: transcendent consciousness, immanent consciousness and manifesting energy. That is, we are resting in the awareness of our own purely spiritual being and at the same time we are aware of our own existence within relativity, that is an extension of our own self as vibratory energy (shakti).

No one is, or can be, either mortal or sinful by nature. Rather, just as all the waves are formed of the ocean and are an inherent, inseparable part of the ocean, so all individuals or jivas are eternal parts of Brahman, the whole. Although Brahman is the totality of our being and existence, no jiva can claim to be the totality of Brahman.

Nevertheless, each jiva is totally divine. Any experience or condition that contradicts or veils this is illusory (maya), and can be eradicated from the consciousness by the practice of yoga as revealed to and formulated by the ancient sages (rishis) of India such as Patanjali. Realization of one's innate divinity is inevitable for each person (jiva).

Just as Ishwara is clothed in the evolving universe of many levels–physical, astral, and causal–so we are clothed in the various energy levels, prakriti or shakti, that are usually called "bodies." As human beings we presently have five bodies (coverings or koshas): the annamaya, pranamaya, manomaya, jnanamaya, and anandamaya koshas. The annamaya body is the physical body formed of atomic matter. The pranamaya body consists of neurological and biomagnetic energies and is the seat of the emotions. The manomaya body is the energy field that is the sensory or perceiving mind. The jnanamaya body is the even subtler energy field that is the intellect (also called the buddhi). The anandamaya body is the primal energy that manifests as the will. All of these have many more aspects than outlined here, and they all consist of many layers within themselves, very much like an onion. All are composed of our personal energy field and are pervaded by our objective consciousness that corresponds to Ishwara as distinguished from our subjective consciousness that corresponds to Brahman.

In the Mundaka Upanishad (3.1.1) it is stated that the human being is like a fruit tree in which two birds are sitting. One bird is eating the fruit of the tree while the other witnesses and actually experiences the other's eating. The tree and its fruit are our bodies; the bird that eats the fruit is the aspect of our consciousness that is involved in external experience; and the other bird is the silent witness aspect of our consciousness untouched by all phenomena: perceiving all but perceived by none but itself and Brahman/Ishwara. This simile also can be applied to Satchidananda.

It should be understood that Brahman, especially as Ishwara, is conscious of creation and we are conscious of our bodies and the creation with which they come into contact, because creation and our bodies are actually themselves consciousness: extensions of Brahman/Ishwara and us. Although often appearing (acting) as inert and unconscious, the energy of which all things consist is intelligent consciousness. This is essential for our understanding of the who and the what of ourselves as well as our reactions to all things.

The spirits and their energies exist eternally in Brahman, within the very heart or depths of the Infinite Consciousness that is Brahman. But, since we are image-reflections of Brahman-Ishwara whose very nature is action through the evolving creation, we, too, seek to evolve beyond our innate finite scope of consciousness in order to develop the capacity to experience infinite consciousness, the very consciousness of Brahman. We cannot become Brahman, but through the evolution of our various bodies we can develop the ability to share in the limitless being and consciousness that is the essential being of Brahman. We can come to see with the eye of Brahman, to hear with the ear of Brahman, to think with the mind of Brahman, and to know with the consciousness of Brahman.

To accomplish this the individual soul comes out from the depths of Brahman and enters into the creation, the dynamic life that is Mahashakti. In this way it begins, through a series of rebirths, a seemingly infinite chain of manifestation-embodiments, evolving through increasingly complex forms to expand its consciousness and its innate capacity for experience, until it reaches the point where it can consciously re-enter the realm of Brahman and participate fully in the divine omnipresence, omniscience, and omnipotence. The spirit thus becomes totally godlike, but in no way does it become God. It becomes *one* with Brahman, but it does not become the *same* as Brahman. A soul that has attained this state is rightly called a Son of God. And if such a one returns to earth to help others to attain the same status he is an Avatara, a Divine Incarnation.

World-view

Dharma includes a God-and-spirit-centric view of the world which affirms that all experiences of enlightenment and divine contact are open to every single human being; that no historical event of spiritual illumination and revelation is unique and unrepeatable *if it is authentic*.

Further, that every spiritual aspirant who follows the path of yoga can verify for himself the truth or error of any statement of belief or unbelief, that blind acceptance of any tenet or individual as a source of spiritual knowledge is spiritually destructive, including demands of exclusivity for any religion or teacher.

Identity with Brahman

Each individual consciousness or jiva not only exists within Brahman, Brahman is the inmost reality of each jiva. Seated within the heart of all, Brahman directs and brings about the awakening of each one. Although in our present state most persons require some kind of instruction and guidance from those who are more experienced in the path of yoga and dharma, it is God alone that enables and enlightens the jiva.

There is no one that can stand in the place of God and claim to represent God in our lives. As Buddha said, a true and worthy teacher (acharya) is only a finger pointing to the moon. God, and none other, is the moon, and the wise do not keep looking at the finger but focus attention on the moon.

Further, there is no philosophical or dogmatic formulation, no intellectual teaching or teacher, that is absolutely necessary for liberation (moksha), the only true salvation. Yoga, however, is necessary because it alone reveals and establishes us in our eternal nature. Moksha is our eternal nature and God is our eternal guru.

Three fundamental facts

There are three fundamental facts of our present existence:
1. Karma: the law of cause and effect, or action and reaction, expounded to us by the rishis.
2. Karma renders necessary the experience of rebirth or reincarnation (punarjanma) in order for the individual to reap the effects of his karmic sowing in past, present, and future births. This, too, is a Law.

3. The purpose or effect of Karma and Rebirth is evolution of consciousness, the unfoldment of the jiva's inherent divinity. At first this takes place automatically, a virtual function of the cosmos (samsara), but in time the human status is reached after passing through countless lower forms of manifestation. After some time the human being becomes capable of taking charge of and accelerating his evolution through the methodology of yoga.

To accommodate these three preceding points, the cosmos perpetually passes through stages of manifestation and non-manifestation, the Days and Nights of Brahma (see Bhagavad Gita 8:16-19). Furthermore, the cosmos is not just physical, but embraces many levels or layers of evolution and consciousness, through which every single jiva passes in its journey to the revelation of its pure nature as eternal Brahman.

The soul and its destiny

The nature of the individual spirit is as much an incomprehensible mystery to the intellect as is the nature of Brahman. This is because both are eternal–and therefore beyond the grasp of the temporal intellect–and both are one. The nature of that oneness is equally incomprehensible. Throughout the ages many people have pointlessly wrangled with one another over definitions of this oneness which by its very nature is indefinable.

The existence of the individual spirit is rooted in Brahman, the infinite Spirit; Brahman is Itself the root of the individual spirit's existence. Yet a distinction exists. Brahman encompasses all individual spirits, but none encompass It. Brahman and the individual spirit are not two, but one. Yet there is a distinction between them. The great Master Tung-Shan, founder of the Soto school of Zen Buddhism, wrote:

If you look for the truth outside yourself,
    it gets farther and farther away.

Today, walking alone, I meet him everywhere I step.
    He is the same as me, yet I am not him.
Only if you understand it in this way
    will you merge with the way things are.

(Note how theistic this poem is, despite the modern insistence that Zen is atheistic.)

As has been said, this status is simply incomprehensible. There is eternal unity and there is eternal diversity. Yet this diversity is not in any sense a duality. The individual spirits are absolutely and irrevocably inseparable from Brahman. There is the beginningless and endless existence of Brahman and all spirits. There is also the distinction-within-unity that is the present and eternal status of the individualized spirits in relation to Brahman. There was never a time when the individualized spirits did not exist as individualized spirits, nor at any time in the future shall this mode of existence cease to be, as Krishna states in the Bhagavad Gita (2:12). What shall cease to be is the limitation of consciousness when the individual spirits attain perfect unity with Brahman/Ishwara in the sharing of Its omniscience, omnipresence, and omnipotence.

Simple as it is, Swami Dayananda Saraswati's statement regarding the status of the sons of God is perhaps the best: "They consciously live and move freely and without limit within God."

The Three are One

Although we have been speaking of various aspects of the threefold nature of God, man and manifestation, from the standpoint of the Absolute these three are one in an incomprehensible manner, though from the standpoint of the individual soul these three are distinct from one another. The Ocean of Brahman is one, but the waves of creation and the souls are many. The great non-dual philosopher Shankaracharya wrote: "O Lord, although we are one, I belong to You, but You do not belong to me. For the ocean can say 'I am the wave,' but the wave cannot say 'I am the ocean.'" Yogananda used to say that we can say "God has become me," but we cannot say "I am God." Accordingly, the viewpoints of Advaita (Non-dualism), Vashistadvaita (Qualified Non-dualism), and Dwaita (Dualism) are all three true when taken together, but if one of them is ignored or overemphasized error is the result. Furthermore, no one of the three is *the* right, best, or highest view. For ultimately all viewing vanishes into Being.

This entire process of evolution that has been set forth above is possible only through the two laws of reincarnation and karma.

Reincarnation

"As Jesus passed by, he saw a man which was blind from his birth. And his disciples asked him, saying, Master, who did sin, this man, or his parents, that he was born blind? Jesus answered, Neither hath this man sinned, nor his parents: but that the works of God should be made manifest in him" (John 9:1-3).

In this passage we learn that the Apostles and Jesus believed that a person's situation in life is determined by his actions—in this case seemingly negative—committed before birth: that is, in a previous life. Although the man's blindness was for the glory of God, Jesus said, "neither hath this man sinned, nor his parents," implying that the man had certainly existed, and been capable of sinning, before the present birth in which he was blind.

Speaking to a crowd about John the Baptist, Jesus told them: "This is he, of whom it is written, Behold, I send my messenger before thy face, which shall prepare thy way before thee…. And if you will receive it, this is Elias which was for to come" (Matthew 11:10, 14). Later "His disciples asked him, saying, Why then say the scribes that Elias must first come? And Jesus answered and said unto them,… I say to you, that Elias is come already, and they knew him not, but have done unto him whatsoever they listed…. Then the disciples understood that he spake unto them of John the Baptist" (Matthew 17:10, 12, 13).

The purpose of reincarnation is for us to grow and evolve spiritually until we return to the Godhead from whence we came. Each life is the result of the ones preceding it and is shaped accordingly–not in the sense of reward or punishment, but as precise mathematical reaction to our actions in those previous lives. We reap what we sowed in them through the exercise of our free wills. Though we may forget it, we are at all times masters of our destiny and not at all swept along blindly by karma, which is really our own creation.

Equally, if not more important, is the fact that every experience and action in our previous births produces a shaping of our personal energies which manifest mostly as the personality. These shapings, called samskaras, are likened to impressions made in wax or clay that momentarily impart a distinctive shape or character, yet are erased and overwritten with other impressions in an endless succession of changes. So karma and samskara are the two determinants of the quality and character of each reincarnation.

The implication of karma

The individual soul, being endowed with free, creative will according to the divine image, must also shoulder the responsibility for that will–the responsibility being in the form of the irrevocable law: "Whatsoever a man soweth, that shall he also reap" (Galatians 6:7). The law is that we must receive back *whatever* we sow, not just some kind of reaction. This retribution must be in the form of experiencing exactly what we have done to others–no substitute. For the Jesus was not just putting forth a social directive when he said: "Whatsoever ye would that men should do to you, do ye even so to them" (Matthew 7:12). He was simply restating the principle of karma that whatever you do to others will in turn be done to you. Reincarnation is an absolute necessity for us to reap what we have sown.

The twin laws of karma and rebirth as understood in the scriptures of India are the fundamental truths about human existence, and without them no religious or personal philosophy can be either true or viable.

Jesus, a siddha

Jesus did not claim to be God, only a son of God as are all sentient beings. As explained earlier, Jesus of Nazareth was not an orthodox Jew, but an Essene who had studied some of the wisdom of India in the Essene schools. He then spent most of his life in India and returned to Israel as a missionary of Sanatana Dharma. This book could not really be a presentation of original Christianity if it did not present the teachings of the Dharma which Jesus brought back from India.

Jesus Christ was God in the sense that as atmas we are all divine, but he was not the Creator God, nor was he a blood sacrifice to satisfy an angry God and draw his wrath away from humanity. Rather, he was a great siddha, a liberated being who for all practical purposes can be called an avatara, an incarnation of God, as have been many others throughout history, especially in India.

Where can we find the authentic teachings of Jesus? In the Upanishads, Bhagavad Gita and Yoga Sutras. Although there are fragments and hints of Jesus' teachings in the Bible, the four Gospels were written long after Jesus and his disciples had departed this world, and a great deal of his teaching is omitted or distorted and even fabricated. The book known as the Gospel of Thomas certainly presents his authentic teachings, and so do some of the texts of the Christian Gnostics found in Egypt.

What then?

If someone accepts the truth that: 1) Jesus had lived most of his life in India before returning to Israel to teach what he had learned (and spiritually realized) there, 2) that after his martyrdom by the religious and civil authorities his guru Sri Chetan Nath brought him back to life, and 3) he returned to India where he lived the rest of his life in the Western Himalayas, though occasionally visiting his disciple Thomas in Kerala, and therefore wishes to be a disciple of Jesus, what should he do? Only what Jesus did before him: become an adherent of Sanatana

Dharma with his whole heart and become a yogi and dedicate his life to attaining Self-realization: Atma jnana leading to Brahmajnana. Then alone will he be a follower of Jesus–by becoming exactly what he was.

What if?

What if someone feels an intense attraction and attachment to Jesus, even though they adopt Sanatana Dharma, practice yoga meditation and seek Self-realization? There is nothing wrong with that, for Jesus is a Master because of those very things. An attraction to Jesus naturally rises from his status as a perfected Son of God, a Siddha, and it also may be a result of past life involvement with Christianity. I have known Indian Brahmins who had devotion to Jesus and kept his picture in their homes, though not becoming Christians. In his youth one of my Brahmin friends felt such an attraction to Jesus that he went to a Roman Catholic priest and asked how he could become a Christian. The priest asked if he had really studied Hinduism. When said he had not, the priest told him to make a serious and deep study of Hinduism and then decide if he wanted to become a Christian. After he followed the priest's advice he was no longer interesting in changing religions, but he kept a picture of Jesus in his puja room and worshipped it daily. There is no reason why a Westerner cannot do the same. And I would certainly advise such a person to study the *Aquarian Gospel of Jesus the Christ* to learn the truth about Jesus and his teachings, as well as *The Second Coming of Christ, Autobiography of a Yogi, Man's Eternal Quest, The Divine Romance* and *Journey to Self-realization* by Yogananda.

INDIAN MASTERS WHO CONSIDERED JESUS ONE OF THEM

The day our *Original Christianity and Original Yoga* website was launched we received an irate communication from one of those Western "Hindus" that believe they are more truly Hindu if they hate other religions—especially Christianity—and deny that Jesus ever existed. But if Jesus did not exist, and is alien to Sanatana Dharma, how is it that great spiritual masters of India have seen him in visions, researched and proved not only his existence but his having lived in India, and expounded his teachings as being the same as (not just consistent with) Sanatana Dharma? I have already cited some of them, but there are more.

Sri Ramakrishna, his great disciple Swami Brahmananda, Swami Rama Tirtha, Swami (Papa) Ramdas, and Paramhansa Yogananda all saw Jesus in visions—some more than once, and some actually spoke with him. Sri Ramakrishna kept a picture of Jesus in his room at the Dakshineswar Kali Temple. He also told several of his disciples that he had seen in visions that they had been disciples of Jesus. Both Swami Rama Tirtha and Swami Ramdas had visions of Jesus while staying at Vashishtha Guha north of Rishikesh in the cave where Jesus had lived for a while (though they did not know that fact at the time of their visions, but learned it later).

Sri Ramakrishna
1836-1886

Paramhansa Yogananda
1893–1952

Swami Brahmananda
1863 – 1922

Swami Rama Tirtha
1873 – 1906

Papa Ramdas
1984 – 1963

Swami Abhedananda and Swami Trigunatitananda, disciples of Sri Ramakrishna, at separate times journeyed to Ladakh and verified the existence of ancient Buddhist texts recording the life of Jesus. Swami Trigunatitananda was also shown two paintings of Jesus by the Buddhist monks, and had a copy of one made from his memory when he was living in America as a Vedanta missionary (see page 16). Swami

Abhedananda, also for a while a Vedanta Missionary to America, printed a translation of the part of the Buddhist text on Jesus and defied the British government's ban on Nicholas Notovitch's *Unknown Life of Jesus Christ* which contained the complete text. He not only brought copies of the book from America to india, he had an edition printed in India. He also wrote the pamphlet: *Why a Hindu Accepts Christ and Rejects Churchianity.*

Swami Abhedananda

Swami Saradananda

A friend of mine gave me a copy of a letter Sri Ramakrishna's disciple Swami Saradananda wrote to her aunt, Edith Grey, who had gone to India and become a disciple of Sri Ma Sarada Devi, the consort of Sri Ramakrishna. Miss Grey had written to the Swami about how she felt equal devotion to Sri Ramakrishna and Jesus. The Swami wrote back: "Our Master assured us that they were just the same."

Later in the twentieth century the Shankaracharya of Puri, Jagadguru Bharata Krishna Tirtha, found what he called "proof positive" of Jesus actually having lived in the Govardhan Math, the present math of the Order of Shankara in Puri. He even wrote a book on the subject, which he found had been thrown away by an illiterate servant when he returned from his world tour, and which he did not live long enough to rewrite.

Before that, Swami Sri Yukteswar Giri, the guru of Yogananda, wrote a study in which he proved that Jesus had lived in India and that his teachings were identical with the Sanatana Dharma which he adopted

and preached in the West. That was borrowed by a Christian missionary who refused, in Sri Yukteswar's lifetime and even after his death, to
return it.

Paramhansa Yogananda wrote and
lectured extensively on the teachings of
Jesus. At his very first speech given in this
country he announced that he would be
holding classes in Boston which would
consist of three half-hour periods each: one
on the teachings of the Bhagavad Gita, one
on the teachings of the Gospels, and one
demonstrating that their teachings were
the same. His two-volume commentary on
the Gospels, *The Second Coming of Christ*,
is perhaps the only complete and reliable
presentation of Jesus' real teachings–which

Paramhansa Yogananda

are mostly unknown to Churchianity. In the forty-ninth chapter of his
Autobiography of a Yogi Yogananda tells of a vision he had of Jesus in his
Encinitas hermitage.

Swami Prabhavananda of the Hollywood Vedanta Society wrote *The
Sermon on the Mount According to Vedanta*
and often referred to Jesus in his lectures.

Swami Akhilananda of the Boston
Vedanta Society wrote a valuable study
called *Hindu View of Christ* and also
cited Jesus as a spiritual authority. (Both
Vedanta Societies celebrated Christmas,
too, as does Belur Math, the world head-
quarters of Ramakrishna Mission.)

As a final example which I witnessed
myself, my beloved Swami Sivananda,
founder of the Divine Life Society in

Swami Sivananda

Rishikesh and perfect example of Sanatana Dharma, not only wrote and published a life of Jesus for popular circulation and celebrated Christmas each year, in the daily evening satsang kirtan he led us all in singing: "O my Jesus, O my Jesus, Lord Jesus: Come, come to me! O my Mary, Mother Mary, Virgin Mary: Come, come to me!" And often at the end, along with other exclamations in praise of Dharma, would call out: "Jesus Bhagavan: ki jai!"

All these great yogis of India did not just believe Jesus existed, they honored him as a liberated son of God and considered him a Sanatana Dharmi just like themselves. And we must not forget that the Nath Yogis consider Jesus as a Nath Yogi and one of their gurus.

APPENDIX TWO:

THE YOGA OF THE NATH YOGIS AND JESUS

Jesus, Sri Ishanath, was a Nath Yogi and therefore practiced the traditional Yoga of the Nath Sampradaya known as Soham Yoga or Soham Sadhana. The following is the text of *Soham Yoga: An Introduction.*

Some history

Yoga is an eternal science intended to reveal and manifest the Eternal. Although the identity of the Supreme Self (Paramatma) and the individual Self (jivatma) with Soham is indicated in the Isha Upanishad (16) and the Brihadaranyaka Upanishad (1.4.1) respectively, no one knows exactly when it was that the knowledge of Soham Yoga was revealed in the world, but the following we do know.

A young man was wandering in the mountains somewhere in India—most likely in the Western Himalayas. He had seen no one else for a very long time, but one day he heard the faint sound of a human voice. Following it, he saw from a distance some people seated together near a river. Slipping into the water, he began swimming toward them. All along the river on that side thick reeds were growing so he was not seen as he stealthily made his way closer.

Soon he began to understand what was being said. Fascinated by the speaker's words he came as close as he dared and for a long time

63

remained absorbed in the amazing things being spoken. For the science of yoga was being expounded by a master to his disciples. Then he heard the master say: "There is a 'fish' in the reeds over there, listening to everything I am saying. Why doesn't he come out and join us?" He did as suggested and became a resident of the master's ashram and learned both philosophy and Soham Yoga.

After diligent practice of meditation for quite some time, the master asked him to return to the plains and teach that yoga to whomever would listen. He was given a new name, Matsyendranath. (Matsyendra means Indra Among Fish and Nath means Master. Indra is king of the gods.) We have no knowledge of what the master's name was. Matsyendranath and his disciples only referred to him as Adi Nath–Original/ First Master. Some believe Adi Nath was Shiva himself manifested to teach yoga, or perhaps the primeval master Bhagavan Sanatkumara, about whom the Brihadaranyaka Upanishad says: "To such a one who has his stains wiped away, Bhagavan Sanatkumara shows the further shore of darkness" (7.26.2).

Matsyendra wandered throughout India, teaching those who were awakened enough to desire and comprehend the yogic path. One day in his wanderings he came to a house where the owner's wife gave him something to eat and a request: that he would bless her to have a child. In response he blessed her and gave her some ashes from a sacred fire, telling her to swallow them. Then he left. The woman followed his instructions and soon conceived and gave birth to a male child. Several years later Matsyendra came there again and saw the little boy outside the house. He told him to bring his mother, and when she came he asked if she remembered him, which she did. Pointing to the boy, he said: "That is my child. I have come for him." The woman agreed and Matsyendra left with the boy, whom he named Gorakhsha, Protector/ Guardian of Light.

Goraksha in time became Gorakshanath (usually called Gorakhnath), the greatest yogi in India's recorded history. In every part of India there are stories told of his living in those areas. He also lived in Nepal, Tibet, Ladakh, and Bhutan. There are shrines and temples to him in all those countries, both Hindu and Buddhist. His major temple is in Gorakhpur, the birthplace of Paramhansa Yogananda, whose younger brother, Sananda, was originally named Goraksha. Considering all the lore about him, Gorakhnath must have lived at least two or three hundred years, and there are many who claim that he has never left his body but is living right now in the Himalayas.

Gorakhnath had many disciples, a large number of them attaining enlightenment. They were the first members of the Nath Yogi Sampradaya, which in time numbered in its ranks the great sage Patanjali, founder of the Yoga Philosophy (Yoga Darshan) and author of the Yoga Sutras, and Jesus of Nazareth (Sri Ishanath). For many centuries the majority of monks in India were Nath Yogis, but in the nineteenth century there was a sharp decline in their numbers, which continues today. However there are several groups of "Nath Panthis" that follow the philosophy and yoga of Matsyendranath and Gorakhnath, and therefore are involved with Soham as the heart of their sadhana.

Soham

Soham means: I Am That. It is the natural vibration of the Self, which occurs spontaneously with each incoming and outgoing breath. By becoming aware of it on the conscious level by mentally repeating it in time with the breath (*So* when inhaling and *Ham* when exhaling), a yogi experiences the identity between his individual Self and the Supreme Self.

According to the Nath Yogis (see my book *Soham Yoga*) Soham has existed within the depths of God from eternity; and the same is true of every sentient being. Soham, then, will reveal our inner being. By meditating on Soham we discover our Self, within which Soham has existed forever. The simple intonation of Soham in time with the breath will do everything in the unfolding of the yogi's spiritual consciousness.

The practice is very simple, and the results very profound. Truly wondrous is the fact that Soham Yoga can go on all the time, not just during meditation, if we apply ourselves to it. The whole life can become a continuous stream of liberating sadhana. "By the mantra 'Soham' separate the jivatma from the Paramatma and locate the jivatma in the heart" (Devi Bhagavatam 11.8.15).

The important thing about Soham Yoga is that it really works. It only takes perseverance.

The two oldest Upanishads on Soham

The Isha and the Brihadaranyaka are the oldest of the Upanishads, giving us the earliest record of Soham that we know.

The Isha Upanishad concludes with four mantras that are to be recited by a dying person to ensure his ascension to the solar world upon leaving his body. (These mantras are also recited by those who attend the cremation of the body.) The sixteenth verse says: "O Pushan, the sole seer, O Controller, O Sun, offspring of Prajapati, spread forth your rays and gather up your radiant light that I may behold you of loveliest form. I am that Purusha [Spirit-Self]: I AM SOHAM." (The Sanskrit text is: *Yo sav asau purushah; soham asmi.*) At the core of every sentient being Soham exists as the Self–*is* the Self. *Soham asmi* literally means "I AM THAT I AM," which is exactly what God told Moses was his Name (Exodus 3:14).

The Brihadaranyaka Upanishad (5.15.2) repeats the identical words. It earlier says: "In the beginning this (world) was only the Self [Atman], in the shape of a person. Looking around he saw nothing else than the Self. He first said, 'I am Soham [*Soham asmi*]'" (1.4.1) Thus Soham is the "first speaking" of the Absolute Itself: the expression of the knowledge and knowing of the Self. Soham is the Name (Embodiment) of the Primeval Being, the Self of the Universe and the Self of our Selfs. Soham is the Consciousness of Brahman and of the Self of each one of us. We, too, are Soham.

The ancient yogis of India discovered that the root impulse of inhalation makes the subtle sound of *So*, and the root impulse of exhalation makes the subtle sound of *Hum* (written as *Ham* in Sanskrit). Since all creation is the thought or ideation of God, meaning is inherent in everything, including the breath: "That [*So*] I am [*Ham*]." In this way every living being is perpetually intoning Soham (Sohum) at the core of their being, saying: I AM THAT: the spirit-Self which is a divine part of the Divine Infinite.

No matter how many ages we wander in forgetfulness of our divine origin and nature, we are always affirming "I am That" without ceasing at each breath. But we have lost the awareness of that sacred thread of inmost knowledge and are now wandering without direction or discernment. But by mentally intoning Soham in time with the breath–*So* when inhaling and *Ham* when exhaling–we consciously take hold of the thread and begin moving in the right direction.

Repeating Soham in a constant flow with the breath turns the mind inward and produces spiritual awareness in an ever-increasing degree. So whenever we intone Soham in time with the breath, we align and link our consciousness with its origin: both our spirit and Divine Spirit.

For the repetition of Soham to produce its effect it must be pronounced correctly. Soham is pronounced like our English words *So* and *Hum*. The short a in Sanskrit is pronounced like the u in *up* or *hunt*, so we say "hum" even though we write it as "ham."

It is most important to pronounce the *O* correctly. It should be pronounced like the long *o* in the Italian or common American manner–as in home and lone. In England, Canada, and parts of the American South, the long *o* is sometimes pronounced as a diphthong, like two vowels jammed together: either like "*ay*-oh" or "*eh*-oh." This is not the correct manner of pronouncing the *O*, which should be a single, pure vowel sound.

The same is true of the *U* in *ham* (hum). As already pointed out, it is pronounced like the u in *up* or *hunt*–not like the u in *truth* or *push*, as is done in parts of Great Britain.

A mantra is most effective if it is mentally intoned—that is, mentally "sung"—on a single note. (The pitch does not matter—whatever is spontaneous and natural.) This makes the repetition stronger and of deeper effect, because intoning unifies the mind and naturally concentrates it.

The Practice of Soham Yoga Meditation

1. Sit upright, comfortable and relaxed, with your hands on your knees or thighs or resting, one on the other, in your lap.

2. Turn your eyes slightly downward and close them gently. This removes visual distractions and reduces your brain-wave activity by about seventy-five percent, thus helping to calm the mind. During meditation your eyes may move upward and downward naturally of their own accord. This is as it should be when it happens spontaneously. But start out with them turned slightly downward without any strain.

3. Be aware of your breath naturally (automatically) flowing in and out. Your mouth should be closed so that all breathing is done through the nose. This also aids in quieting the mind. Though your mouth is closed, the jaw muscles should be relaxed so the upper and lower teeth are not clenched or touching one another, but parted. Breathe naturally, spontaneously. Your breathing should always be easeful and natural, not deliberate or artificial.

4. Then in a very quiet and gentle manner begin *mentally* intoning Soham in time with your breathing. (Remember: Soham is pronounced like our English words *So* and *Hum*.)

   Intone *Soooooo*, prolonging a single intonation throughout each inhalation, and *Huuummm*, prolonging a single intonation throughout each exhalation, "singing" the syllables on a single note.

   There is no need to pull or push the mind. Let your relaxed attention sink into and get absorbed in the mental sound of your inner intonings of Soham.

Fit the intonations to the breath—not the breath to the intonations. If the breath is short, then the intonation should be short. If the breath is long, then the intonation should be long. It does not matter if the inhalations and exhalations are not of equal length. Whatever is natural and spontaneous is what is right.

Your intonation of *Soooooo* should begin when your inhalation begins, and *Huuummm* should begin when your exhalation begins. In this way your intonations should be virtually continuous, that is:

SooooooHuuummmSooooooHuuummmSooooooHuuummmSooooooHuuummm.

Do not torture yourself about this—basically continuous is good enough.

5. For the rest of your meditation time keep on intoning Soham in time with your breath, calmly listening to the mental sound.

6. In Soham meditation we do not deliberately concentrate on any particular point of the body such as the third eye, as we want the subtle energies of Soham to be free to manifest themselves as is best at the moment. However, as you meditate you may become aware of one or more areas of your brain or body at different times. This is all right when such sensations come and go spontaneously, but keep centered on your intonations of Soham in time with your breath.

7. In time your inner mental intonations of Soham may change to a more mellow or softer form, even to an inner whispering that is almost silent, but the syllables are always fully present and effective. Your intonations may even become silent, like a soundless mouthing of Soham or just the thought or movement of Soham, yet you will still be intoning Soham in your intention. And of this be sure: Soham never ceases. Never. You may find that your intonations of Soham move back and forth from more objective to more subtle and back to more objective. Just intone in the manner that is natural at the moment.

8. In the same way you will find that your breath will also become more subtle and refined, and slow down. Sometimes the breath may not be perceived as movement of the lungs, but just as the subtle pranic energy movement which causes the physical breath. Your breath can even become so light that it seems as though you are not breathing at all, just *thinking* the breath (or almost so).

9. Thoughts, impressions, memories, inner sensations, and suchlike may also arise during meditation. Be calmly aware of all these things in a detached and objective manner, but keep your attention centered in your intonations of Soham in time with your breath. Do not let your attention become centered on or caught up in any inner or outer phenomena. Be calmly aware of all these things in a detached and objective manner. They are part of the transforming work of Soham, and are perfectly all right, but keep your attention centered in your intonations of Soham in time with your breath. Even though something feels very right or good when it occurs, it should not be forced or hung on to. The sum and substance of it all is this: It is not the experience we are after, but the effect. Also, since we are all different, no one can say exactly what a person's experiences in meditation are going to be like.

10. Soham japa and meditation can make us aware of the subtle levels of our being, many of which are out of phase with one another and are either confused or reversed in their polarity. The japa and meditation correct these things, but sometimes, especially at the beginning of meditation, we can experience these aberrations as uncomfortable or uneasy sensations, a feeling or heaviness or stasis or other peculiar sensations that are generally uncomfortable and somehow feel "not right." When this occurs, do not try to interfere with it or "make it better." Rather, just relax, keep on with the japa/meditation, calmly aware and let it be as it is. In time the problem in the subtle energy levels will be corrected and the feeling will become easy and pleasant. Simple

as the practice is, it has deep and far-reaching effects, as you will see for yourself.

11. If you find yourself getting restless, distracted, fuzzy, anxious or tense in any degree, just take a deep breath and let it out fully, feeling that you are releasing and breathing out all tensions, and continue as before.

12. Remember: Soham Yoga meditation basically consists of four things: a) sitting with the eyes closed; b) being aware of our breath as it moves in and out; c) mentally intoning Soham in time with the breath; and d) listening to those mental intonations: all in a relaxed and easeful manner, without strain.

    Breath and sound are the two major spiritual powers possessed by us, so they are combined for Soham Yoga practice. It is very natural to intone Soham in time with the breathing. It is simple and easy.

13. At the end of your meditation time, keep on intoning Soham in time with your breath as you go about your various activities, listening to the inner mantric sound, just as in meditation. One of the cardinal virtues of Soham sadhana is its capacity to be practiced throughout the day. The *Yoga Rasyanam* in verse 303 says: "Before and after the regular [meditation] practice, the repetition of Soham should be continuously done [in time with the breath] while walking, sitting or even sleeping.... This leads to ultimate success."

Can it be that simple and easy? Yes, because it goes directly to the root of our bondage which is a single–and therefore simple–thing: loss of awareness. Soham is the seed (bija) mantra of nirvanic consciousness. You take a seed, put it in the soil, water it and the sun does the rest. You plant the seed of Soham in your inner consciousness through japa and meditation and both your Self and the Supreme Self do the rest. By intentionally intoning *So* and *Ham* with the breath we are linking the conscious with superconscious mind, bringing the superconscious onto the conscious level and merging them until they become one. It is divinely simple!

Soham Yoga Sadhana in three sentences

The two supreme yogis of India's history, Matsyendranath and Gorakhnath, and the Yoga Chudamani Upanishad have made three statements that are most important for the yogi, for they present the essence of Soham Sadhana.

1. The inhalation comes in with the subtle sound of *So*, and the exhalation goes out with the subtle sound of *Ham*.
2. There is no knowledge equal to this, nor has there ever been in the past or shall be in the future any knowledge equal to this.
3. There is no japa equal to this, nor has there ever been in the past or shall be in the future any japa equal to this.

The implication is that the unequaled, and therefore supreme, knowledge and the unequaled and supreme yoga practice are the mental intonations of *So* throughout the inhalation and *Ham* throughout the exhalation. And therefore that intoning *So* and *Ham* in time with the breath is the totality of Soham Yoga practice.

Such gimmicks as thinking the breath is going up the spine with the intonation of *So* and down the spine with the intonation of *Ham*, or intoning Soham at the chakras, are not Soham Sadhana. Consequently, the Soham yogi's attention should be only on the movement of his breath and his mental intonations of *So* and *Ham* in time with it.

These three statements of Matsyendranath, Gorakhnath and the Yoga Chudamani Upanishad also imply that the difference between Soham Yoga and other yogas is the difference between lightning and lightning bugs.

How is this? Because, as we have seen in the previous chapter, according to the Isha and Brihadaranyaka Upanishads the fundamental nature of both the Supreme Self (Ishwara) and the Individual Self (Jiva) of each one of us, is Soham. Soham Sadhana takes us directly and immediately into the consciousness of the Self and the Supreme Self, simultaneously. Other yoga practices do not do this, but go about it in a roundabout manner, taking many years (if not decades) before even beginning to do what Soham Sadhana does from the very first.

In Soham Yoga only the sufficient time to experience the full range of Self-experience and become permanently established in that experience is necessary for the Soham yogi to become liberated. As soon as he truly knows: "I am Soham," the Great Work is complete. For Ishwarapranidhana not only means offering the life to God, it also literally means offering the breath (prana) to God. This is done by intoning *So* during inhalation and *Ham* during exhalation, both in meditation and the rest of the day and night. In this way Soham Bhava, God-consciousness, is attained.

What can you expect?

Yoga and its practice is a science and the yogi is the laboratory in which that science is applied and tested. At first the aspirant takes the word of a book, a teacher or other aspirants that a yoga method is worthwhile, but eventually it is his personal experience alone that should determine his evaluation of any yoga practice. Because each person is unique in his makeup there can be a tremendous difference in each one's experience of yoga. Nevertheless, there are certain principles which can be stated.

If a yogi is especially sensitive or has practiced the method in a previous life, he may get obviously beneficial results right away. Yet for many people it takes a while for a practice to take hold and produce a steadily perceptible effect. One yogi I knew experienced satisfactory effects immediately. Then to his puzzlement for some days it seemed that absolutely nothing was happening, that his meditation was a blank. But he had the deep conviction (no doubt from a past life as a yogi) that Soham sadhana was the right and true way for him. So he kept on meditating for hours at a time. Then one morning during the final hour of meditation results began coming in the form of experiences that he had not had before. All doubt was dispelled, and he knew he was on the right track. From then onward everything was satisfactory, though there were alternating periods of active experiences and simple quiet observation of inner rest.

Experiences, as I say, can be different for everyone, but certainly peace and refinement of consciousness can be expected. Many things will occur that simply cannot be described because ordinary human language has no words for them. The real test is the yogi's state of mind outside meditation. This he should watch carefully. And he must make sure that he is always practicing correctly. Fortunately, Soham sadhana is simple and easy to do.

Warning: Do Not Interfere!

We are used to directing and controlling as much of our life as possible. But what applies to the external life as wisdom is not necessarily so in the internal life of meditation. The very simple twelve points given previously when followed exactly in a relaxed and calm manner will produce the inner environment in which Soham can do its divine work of revealing itself as the consciousness that is the yogi's true Self. If there is any interference in the form of trying to change something or direct the meditation or experience in any way, the process is interrupted and will produce no results. Naturally, since the practice is so incredibly simple and we have read all kinds of propaganda about "powerful" yogas and the chills and thrills they produce and the "profound insights" and even visions of higher worlds, etc. and etc. that supposedly result from them, we wonder if there surely isn't "more than this to it" and consider trying out such gimmicks as intoning Soham at the chakras, integrating it with some artificial form of pranayama, concentrating on the spine while visualizing/imagining currents moving up and down the spine, and other "enhancements" that may entertain but will only be obstacles to success in Soham sadhana.

The truth is that Soham intoned in time with the breath immediately begins producing a tremendous number of yogic kriyas, but kriyas that are so subtle and natural that they are usually not perceived. It takes real refinement of the mental energies to experience much of what Soham effects in the entire being of the yogi. I have been astonished at how profound the effects of Soham sadhana are, and some of my experiences have been really incredible, but I have had decades of yogic practice behind me to enable me to experience and understand the workings of Soham. I am not describing any of these experiences lest when you encounter them yourself you wonder if your experience is only auto-suggestion based on my description.

Be wise and just breathe and intone Soham in time with it with eyes closed during meditation and open during the rest of the day's activity. Nothing else, but just being aware of that process and listening to the inner intonations of Soham is the secret and the assurance of success. And that is all. Soham must not be interfered with–it really cannot be, so any attempt will interrupt and spoil the practice and drag you back on the path of samsara, however "yogic" it may seem to you.

Simplicity of practice

The simpler and more easeful the yoga practice, the more deeply effective it is. This is a universal principle in the realm of inner development and experience. How is this? In the inner world of meditation things are often just the opposite to the way they are in the outer world. Whereas in the outer world a strong aggressive force is most effective in producing a change, in the inner world it is subtle, almost minimal force or movement that is most effectual–even supremely powerful. Those familiar with homeopathic medicine will understand the concept that the more subtle an element is, the more potentially effective it is. In meditation and japa the lightest touch is usually the most effective. This being so, the simple subtle intonations of Soham are the strongest and most effective form of mantric invocation.

An incident that took place during one of the crusades illustrates this. At a meeting between the leaders of the European forces and Saladin, commander of the Arab armies, one of the Europeans tried to impress and intimidate Saladin by having one of his soldiers cleave a heavy wooden chair in half with a single downstroke of his broadsword. In response, Saladin ordered someone to toss a silk scarf as light and delicate as a spider's web into the air. As it descended, he simply held his scimitar beneath it with the sharp edge upward. When the scarf touched the edge, it sheared in half and fell on either side of the blade without even a whisper as he held it completely still. This is the power of the subtle and simple practice of Soham Yoga meditation.

Subtlety of practice

Soham sadhana is extraordinarily powerful, yet until we become attuned to it by some time of practice it may seem very mild, just a kind of yogic sitting-up exercise. But it is a mighty tool of yoga alchemy. The secret of its power and effectiveness is its subtlety–the very thing that may cause it to be disregarded and not recognized for its intense value, for it is the subtle energies that are able to work lasting changes in our awareness. The more evolved consciousness or energy becomes, the more refined and subtle it becomes–truly spiritual.

It is the very subtle energies that are able to work lasting changes in our awareness. The more evolved consciousness or energy becomes, the more refined and subtle it becomes. Thus it is the highest level of spiritual powers alone that are able to effect our ascent in consciousness.

Tension of any kind interferes with these energies. It is important, then, to keep in mind that often when things seem stuck in meditation and not moving as they should, or when the mind does not calm down, it is often because we are not relaxed sufficiently and are not allowing our inner intonations of Soham to become as subtle as they should be. For the subtler the intonations, the more effective and on target they are.

Even so, I do not mean to give you the impression that your inner intonations of Soham should become feeble or weak in the sense of becoming tenuous–only barely within your mental grasp, and liable to slip away and leave you blank. Not at all. The inner sound of the intonations may become subtler and subtler, but they do not at all become weaker—only gentler and more profound and therefore more effective.

An exception

In point 6 of the Soham Meditation instructions I said that "we do not deliberately concentrate on any particular point of the body such as the third eye, as we want the subtle energies of Soham to be free to manifest themselves as is best at the moment." There is an exception to that. On occasion, such as at the very beginning of meditation or when during the rest of the day you find your attention drifting from the breath and Soham, it can be helpful to make yourself very gently (lest you give yourself a headache from tension) aware of your entire brain (Sahasrara) area, feeling that the breath and Soham intonations are taking place there.

A short time of this awareness (which can arise spontaneously as well) is sufficient, because correct practice will result in Sahasrara awareness naturally.

There is an entire book on the subject of Soham Yoga entitled: Soham Yoga: The Yoga of the Self, *which we recommend you read.*

DID YOU ENJOY READING THIS BOOK?

Thank you for taking the time to read *The Christ of India*. If you enjoyed it, please consider telling your friends or posting a short review at Amazon, Goodreads, or the book site of your choice.

Word of mouth is an author's best friend and much appreciated.

Get your FREE Meditation Guide

Sign up for the Light of the Spirit Newsletter and get
Learn How to Meditate Effectively.

Get free updates: newsletters, blog posts, and podcasts, plus exclusive content from Light of the Spirit Monastery.

Visit: OCOY.org/signup

GLOSSARY

Acharya: Preceptor; teacher; spiritual teacher/ guide; guru.

Atma(n): The individual spirit or Self that is one with Brahman. The true nature or identity.

Avatar(a): A Divine Incarnation.

Bhagavad Gita: "The Song of God." The sacred philosophical text often called "the Hindu Bible," part of the epic Mahabharata by Vyasa; the most popular sacred text in Hinduism.

Brahman: The Absolute Reality; the Truth proclaimed in the Upanishads; the Supreme Reality that is one and indivisible, infinite, and eternal; all-pervading, changeless Existence; Existence-knowledge-bliss Absolute (Satchidananda); Absolute Consciousness; it is not only all-powerful but all-power itself; not only all-knowing and blissful but all-knowledge and all-bliss itself.

Darshan: Literally "sight" or "seeing;" vision, literal and metaphysical; a system of philosophy (see Sad-darshanas).

Dharma: The righteous way of living, as enjoined by the sacred scriptures and the spiritually illumined; characteristics; law; lawfulness; virtue; righteousness; norm.

Gorakhnath: A master yogi of the Nath Yogi (Siddha Yogi) tradition. His dates are not positively known, but he seems to have lived for many centuries and travelled throughout all of India, Bhutan, Tibet, and Ladakh teaching philosophy and yoga.

Jiva: Individual spirit.

Karma: Karma, derived from the Sanskrit root *kri*, which means to act, do, or make, means any kind of action, including thought and feeling. It also means the effects of action. Karma is both action and reaction, the metaphysical equivalent of the principle: "For every action there is an equal and opposite reaction." "Whatsoever a man soweth, that shall he also reap" (Galatians 6:7). It is karma operating through the law of cause and effect that binds the jiva or the individual soul to the wheel of birth and death. There are three forms of karma: sanchita, agami, and prarabdha. Sanchita karma is the vast store of accumulated actions done in the past, the fruits of which have not yet been reaped. Agami karma is the action that will be done by the individual in the future. Prarabdha karma is the action that has begun to fructify, the fruit of which is being reaped in this life.

Maharishi: Maha-rishi–great sage.

Maya: The illusive power of Brahman; the veiling and the projecting power of the universe, the power of Cosmic Illusion. "The Measurer"–a reference to the two delusive "measures": Time and Space.

Mleccha: Foreigner; an alien; barbarian; non-Aryan; member of an outcast race.

Moksha: Release; liberation; the term is particularly applied to the liberation from the bondage of karma and the wheel of birth and death; Absolute Experience.

Patanjali: A yogi of ancient India, the author of the Yoga Sutras.

Punarjanma: "Birth again;" rebirth/reincarnation.

Purusha: "Person" in the sense of a conscious spirit. Both God and the individual spirits are purushas, but God is the Adi (Original, Archetypal) Purusha, Parama (Highest) Purusha, and the Purushottama (Highest or Best of the Purushas).

Rishi: Sage; seer of the Truth.

Sad-darshanas: The six orthodox systems of Indian philosophy: Nyaya, Vaisheshika, Sankhya, Yoga, Mimamsa, and Vedanta.

Sampradaya: Tradition; philosophical school; literally: "handed-down instruction;" also a line of initiatic empowerment.

Samsara: Life through repeated births and deaths; the wheel of birth and death; the process of earthly life.

Samskara (2): A ritual that makes an impression or change in the individual for whom it is done. There are sixteen samskaras prescribed by the dharma shastras, beginning with conception (garbhadan) and concluding with the rite for the departed soul (antyshthi). The major ones besides these two are the birth rite (jatakarman), naming ceremony (namakaranam), the first eating of solid food (annaprasannam), the first cutting of the hair (chudakaraman), bestowal of the sacred thread and instruction in the Gayatri mantra (upanayanam), marriage (vivahanam), taking up of the retired life (vanaprastha), and taking up the monastic life (sannyasa). They are all done at points in the person's life when significant changes in the subtle energy bodies are going to take place. Thus the samskara protects and strengthens the individual at those times and also prepares him for those changes, making actual alterations in his subtle bodies. Although they are often made social occasions, they are very real instruments of change to facilitate and further the person's personal evolution. They are the linchpins of dharmic life, and essentially spiritual events.

Sanatana: Eternal; everlasting; ancient; primeval.

Sanatana Dharma: "The Eternal Religion," also known as "Arya Dharma," "the religion of those who strive upward [Aryas]." Hinduism.

Sanskrit: The language of the ancient sages of India and therefore of the Indian scriptures and yoga treatises.

Shankara: Shankaracharya; Adi (the first) Shankaracharya: The great reformer and re-establisher of Vedic Religion in India around 300 B.C. He is the unparalleled exponent of Advaita (Non-Dual) Vedanta. He also reformed the mode of monastic life and founded (or regenerated) the ancient Swami Order.

Shaiva/Shaivite: A worshipper of Shiva; pertaining to Shiva.

Shakta: A worshipper of Shakti, the Divine Feminine.

Shaucha: Purity; cleanliness.

Shiva: A name of God meaning "One Who is all Bliss and the giver of happiness to all." Although classically applied to the Absolute Brahman, Shiva can also refer to God (Ishwara) in His aspect of Dissolver and Liberator (often mistakenly thought of as "destroyer").

Shuddhi: The state of purity (shuddha); purification.

Siddha: A perfected–liberated–being, an adept, a seer, a perfect yogi.

Upanishads: Books (of varying lengths) of the philosophical teachings of the ancient sages of India on the knowledge of Absolute Reality. The upanishads contain two major themes: (1) the individual self (atman) and the Supreme Self (Paramatman) are one in essence, and (2) the goal of life is the realization/manifestation of this unity, the realization of God (Brahman). There are eleven principal upanishads: Isha, Kena, Katha, Prashna, Mundaka, Mandukya, Taittiriya, Aitareya, Chandogya, Brihadaranyaka, and Shvetashvatara, all of which were commented on by Shankara, Ramanuja and Madhavacharya, thus setting the seal of authenticity on them.

Vaishnava: A devotee of Vishnu.

Vedas: The oldest scriptures of India, considered the oldest scriptures of the world, that were revealed in meditation to the Vedic Rishis (seers). Although in modern times there are said to be four Vedas (Rig, Sama, Yajur, and Atharva), in the upanishads only three are listed (Rig, Sama, and Yajur). In actuality, there is only one Veda: the Rig Veda. The Sama Veda is only a collection of Rig Veda hymns that are marked (pointed) for singing. The Yajur Veda is a small book giving directions on just one form of Vedic sacrifice. The Atharva Veda is only a collection of theurgical mantras to be recited for the cure of various afflictions or to be recited over the herbs to be taken as medicine for those afflictions.

Vishnu: "The all-pervading;" God as the Preserver.

Yajnopavita: Sacred thread. A triple thread worn by the twice-born (dwijas) that represents the threefold Brahman. It is essential for the performance of all the rites of the twice-born. Usually worn only by Brahmins, originally it was worn by Kshatriyas and Vaishyas as well.

Yama and Niyama: Sometimes called The Ten Commandments of Yoga. Yama consists of five restraint or abstentions: 1) ahimsa–non-violence, non-injury, harmlessness; 2) satya–truthfulness, honesty; 3) asteya–non-stealing, honesty, non-misappropriativeness; 4) brahmacharya–continence; and 5) aparigraha–non-possessiveness, non-greed, non-selfishness, non-acquisitiveness. Niyama consists of five observances: 1) shaucha–purity, cleanliness; 2) santosha–contentment, peacefulness; 3) tapas–austerity, practical (i.e., result-producing) spiritual discipline; 4) swadhyaya–self-study, spiritual study; and 5) Ishwarapranidhana–offering of one's life to God.

Yoga: Literally, "joining" or "union" from the Sanskrit root yuj. Union with the Supreme Being, or any practice that makes for such union. Meditation that unites the individual spirit with God, the Supreme Spirit. The name of the philosophy expounded by the sage Patanjali, teaching the process of union of the individual with the Universal Soul.

Yogananda (Paramhansa): The most influential yogi of the twentieth century in the West, author of *Autobiography of a Yogi* and founder of Self-Realization Fellowship in America.

ABOUT THE AUTHOR

Swami Nirmalananda Giri (Abbot George Burke) is the founder and director of the Light of the Spirit Monastery (Atma Jyoti Ashram) in Cedar Crest, New Mexico, USA.

In his many pilgrimages to India, he had the opportunity of meeting some of India's greatest spiritual figures, including Swami Sivananda of Rishikesh and Anandamayi Ma. During his first trip to India he was made a member of the ancient Swami Order by Swami Vidyananda Giri, a direct disciple of Paramhansa Yogananda, who had himself been given sannyas by the Shankaracharya of Puri, Jagadguru Bharati Krishna Tirtha.

In the United States he also encountered various Christian saints, including Saint John Maximovich of San Francisco and Saint Philaret Voznesensky of New York. He was ordained in the Liberal Catholic Church (International) to the priesthood on January 25, 1974, and consecrated a bishop on August 23, 1975.

For many years Swami Nirmalananda has researched the identity of Jesus Christ and his teachings with India and Sanatana Dharma, including Yoga. It is his conclusion that Jesus lived in India for most of his life, and was a yogi and Sanatana Dharma missionary to the West. After his resurrection he returned to India and lived the rest of his life in the Himalayas.

He has written extensively on these and other topics, many of which are posted at OCOY.org.

Atma Jyoti Ashram
(Light of the Spirit Monastery)

Atma **Jyoti Ashram** (Light of the Spirit Monastery) is a monastic community for those men who seek direct experience of the Spirit through yoga meditation, traditional yogic discipline, Sanatana Dharma and the life of the sannyasi in the tradition of the Order of Shankara. Our lineage is in the Giri branch of the Order.

The public outreach of the monastery is through its website, OCOY.org (Original Christianity and Original Yoga). There you will find many articles on Original Christianity and Original Yoga, including *The Christ of India*. *Foundations of Yoga* and *How to Be a Yogi* are practical guides for anyone seriously interested in living the Yoga Life.

You will also discover many other articles on leading an effective spiritual life, including *Soham Yoga: The Yoga of the Self* and *Spiritual Benefits of a Vegetarian Diet*, as well as the "Dharma for Awakening" series—in-depth commentaries on these spiritual classics: the Bhagavad Gita, the Upanishads, the Dhammapada, the Tao Teh King and more.

You can listen to podcasts by Swami Nirmalananda on meditation, the Yoga Life, and remarkable spiritual people he has met in India and elsewhere, at http://ocoy.org/podcasts/

READING FOR AWAKENING

Light of the Spirit Press presents books on spiritual wisdom and Original Christianity and Original Yoga. From our "Dharma for Awakening" series (practical commentaries on the world's scriptures) to books on how to meditate and live a successful spiritual life, you will find books that are informative, helpful, and even entertaining.

Light of the Spirit Press is the publishing house of Light of the Spirit Monastery (Atma Jyoti Ashram) in Cedar Crest, New Mexico, USA. Our books feature the writings of the founder and director of the monastery, Swami Nirmalananda Giri (Abbot George Burke) which are also found on the monastery's website, OCOY.org.

We invite you to explore our publications in the following pages.

Find out more about our publications at
lightofthespiritpress.com

BOOKS ON MEDITATION

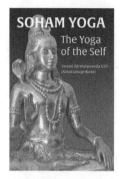

Soham Yoga
The Yoga of the Self

A complete and in-depth guide to effective meditation and the life that supports it, this important book explains with clarity and insight what real yoga is, and why and how to practice Soham Yoga meditation.

Discovered centuries ago by the Nath yogis, this simple and classic approach to self-realization has no "secrets," requires no "initiation," and is easily accessible to the serious modern yogi.

Includes helpful, practical advice on leading an effective spiritual life and many Illuminating quotes on Soham from Indian scriptures and great yogis.

"This book is a complete spiritual path." –Arnold Van Wie

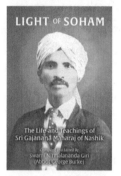

Light of Soham
The Life and Teachings of Sri Gajanana Maharaj of Nashik

Gajanan Murlidhar Gupte, later known as Gajanana Maharaj, led an unassuming life, to all appearances a normal unmarried man of contemporary society. Crediting his personal transformation to the practice of the Soham mantra, he freely shared this practice with a small number of disciples, whom he simply called his friends. Strictly avoiding the trap of gurudom, he insisted that his friends be self-reliant and not be dependent on him for their spiritual progress. Yet he was uniquely able to assist them in their inner development.

The Inspired Wisdom of Gajanana Maharaj
A Practical Commentary on Leading an Effectual Spiritual Life

Presents the teachings and sayings of the great twentieth-century Soham yogi Gajanana Maharaj, with a commentary by Swami Nirmalananda.

The author writes: "In reading about Gajanana Maharaj I encountered a holy personality that eclipsed all others for me. In his words I found a unique wisdom that altered my perspective on what yoga, yogis, and gurus should be.

"But I realized that through no fault of their own, many Western readers need a clarification and expansion of Maharaj's meaning to get the right understanding of his words. This commentary is meant to help my friends who, like me have found his words 'a light in the darkness.'"

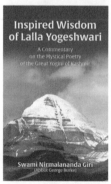

Inspired Wisdom of Lalla Yogeshwari
A Commentary on the Mystical Poetry of the Great Yogini of Kashmir

Lalla Yogeshwari was a great fourteenth-century yogini and wandering ascetic of Kashmir, whose mystic poetry were the earliest compositions in the Kashmiri language. She was in the tradition of the Nath Yogi Sampradaya whose meditation practice is that of Soham Sadhana: the joining of the mental repetition of Soham Mantra with the natural breath.

Swami Nirmalananda's commentary mines the treasures of Lalleshwari's mystic poems and presents his reflections in an easily intelligible fashion for those wishing to put these priceless teachings on the path of yogic self-transformation into practice.

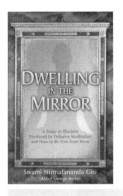

Dwelling in the Mirror
*A Study of Illusions Produced By Delusive Meditation
And How to Be Free from Them*

Swami Nirmalananda says of this book:
"Over and over people have mistaken trivial and pathological conditions for enlightenment, written books, given seminars and gained a devoted following.

"Most of these unfortunate people were completely unreachable with reason. Yet there are those who can have an experience and realize that it really cannot be real, but a vagary of their mind. Some may not understand that on their own, but can be shown by others the truth about it. For them and those that may one day be in danger of meditation-produced delusions I have written this brief study."

BOOKS ON YOGA & SPIRITUAL LIFE

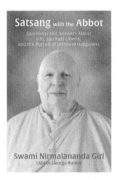

Satsang with the Abbot
*Questions and Answers about Life, Spiritual Liberty,
and the Pursuit of Ultimate Happiness*

The questions in this book range from the most sublime to the most practical. "How can I attain samadhi?" "I am married with children. How can I lead a spiritual life?" "What is Self-realization?" "How important is belief in karma and reincarnation?"

In Swami Nirmalananda's replies to these questions the reader will discover common sense, helpful information, and a guiding light for their journey through and beyond the forest of cliches, contradictions, and confusion of yoga, Hinduism, Christianity, and metaphysical thought.

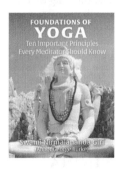

Foundations of Yoga
Ten Important Principles Every Meditator Should Know

An introduction to the important foundation principles of Patanjali's Yoga: Yama and Niyama

Yama and Niyama are often called the Ten Commandments of Yoga, but they have nothing to do with the ideas of sin and virtue or good and evil as dictated by some cosmic potentate. Rather they are determined by a thoroughly practical, pragmatic basis: that which strengthens and facilitates our yoga practice should be observed and that which weakens or hinders it should be avoided.

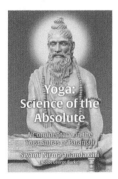

Yoga: Science of the Absolute
A Commentary on the Yoga Sutras of Patanjali

The Yoga Sutras of Patanjali is the most authoritative text on Yoga as a practice. It is also known as the Yoga Darshana because it is the fundamental text of Yoga as a philosophy.

In this commentary, Swami Nirmalananda draws on the age-long tradition regarding this essential text, including the commentaries of Vyasa and Shankara, the most highly regarded writers on Indian philosophy and practice, as well as I. K. Taimni and other authoritative commentators, and adds his own ideas based on half a century of study and practice. Serious students of yoga will find this an essential addition to their spiritual studies.

The Benefits of Brahmacharya
*A Collection of Writings About the Spiritual,
Mental, and Physical Benefits of Continence*

"Brahmacharya is the basis for morality. It is the basis for eternal life. It is a spring flower that exhales immortality from its petals." Swami Sivananda

This collection of articles from a variety of authorities including Mahatma Gandhi, Sri Ramakrishna, Swami Vivekananda, Swamis Sivananda and Chidananda of the Divine Life Society, Swami Nirmalananda, and medical experts, presents many facets of brahmacharya and will prove of immense value to all who wish to grow spiritually.

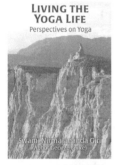

Living the Yoga Life
Perspectives on Yoga

"Dive deep; otherwise you cannot get the gems at the bottom of the ocean. You cannot pick up the gems if you only float on the surface." Sri Ramakrishna

In *Living the Yoga Life* Swami Nirmalananda shares the gems he has found from a lifetime of "diving deep." This collection of reflections and short essays addresses the key concepts of yoga philosophy that are so easy to take for granted. Never content with the accepted cliches about yoga sadhana, the yoga life, the place of a guru, the nature of Brahman and our unity with It, Swami Nirmalananda's insights on these and other facets of the yoga life will inspire, provoke, enlighten, and even entertain.

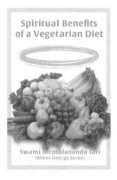

Spiritual Benefits of a Vegetarian Diet

The health benefits of a vegetarian diet are well known, as are the ethical aspects. But the spiritual advantages should be studied by anyone involved in meditation, yoga, or any type of spiritual practice.

Diet is a crucial aspect of emotional, intellectual, and spiritual development as well. For diet and consciousness are interrelated, and purity of diet is an effective aid to purity and clarity of consciousness.

The major thing to keep in mind when considering the subject of vegetarianism is its relevancy in relation to our explorations of consciousness. We need only ask: Does it facilitate my spiritual growth—the development and expansion of my consciousness? The answer is Yes.

BOOKS ON THE SACRED SCRIPTURES OF INDIA

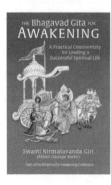

The Bhagavad Gita for Awakening
A Practical Commentary for Leading a Successful Spiritual Life

Drawing from the teachings of Sri Ramakrishna, Jesus, Paramhansa Yogananda, Ramana Maharshi, Swami Vivekananda, Swami Sivananda of Rishikesh, Papa Ramdas, and other spiritual masters and teachers, as well as his own experiences, Swami Nirmalananda illustrates the teachings of the Gita with stories which make the teachings of Krishna in the Gita vibrant and living.

From *Publisher's Weekly*: "[The author] enthusiastically explores the story as a means for knowing oneself, the cosmos, and one's calling within it. His plainspoken insights often distill complex lessons with simplicity and sagacity. Those with a deep interest in the Gita will find much wisdom here."

The Upanishads for Awakening
A Practical Commentary on India's Classical Scriptures

The sacred scriptures of India are vast. Yet they are only different ways of seeing the same thing, the One Thing which makes them both valid and ultimately harmonious. That unifying subject is Brahman: God the Absolute, beyond and besides whom there is no "other" whatsoever. The thirteen major Upanishads are the fountainhead of all expositions of Brahman.

Swami Nirmalananda illumines the Upanishads' practical value for spiritual seekers from the unique perspective of a lifetime of study and practice of both Eastern and Western spirituality.

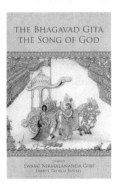

The Bhagavad Gita–The Song of God

Often called the "Bible" of Hinduism, the Bhagavad Gita is found in households throughout India and has been translated into every major language of the world. Literally billions of copies have been handwritten or printed.

The clarity of this translation by Swami Nirmalananda makes for easy reading, while the rich content makes this the ideal "study" Gita. As the original Sanskrit language is so rich, often there are several accurate translations for the same word, which are noted in the text, giving the spiritual student the needed understanding of the fullness of the Gita.

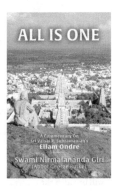

All Is One
A Commentary On Sri Vaiyai R. Subramanian's Ellam Ondre

"I you want moksha, read and practice the instructions in Ellam Ondre." –Ramana Maharshi

Swami Nirmalananda's insightful commentary brings even further light to Ellam Ondre's refreshing perspective on what Unity signifies, and the path to its realization.

Written in the colorful and well-informed style typical of his other commentaries, it is a timely and important contribution to Advaitic literature that explains Unity as the fruit of yoga sadhana, rather than mere wishful thinking or some vague intellectual gymnastic, as is so commonly taught by the modern "Advaita gurus."

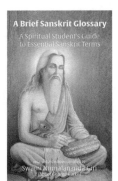

A Brief Sanskrit Glossary
A Spiritual Student's Guide to Essential Sanskrit Terms

This Sanskrit glossary contains full translations and explanations of hundreds of the most commonly used spiritual Sanskrit terms, and will help students of the Bhagavad Gita, the Upanishads, the Yoga Sutras of Patanjali, and other Indian scriptures and philosophical works to expand their vocabularies to include the Sanskrit terms contained in these, and gain a fuller understanding in their studies.

The Christ of India
The Story of Original Christianity

"Original Christianity" is the teaching of both Jesus and his Apostle Saint Thomas in India. Although it was new to the Mediterranean world, it was really the classical, traditional teachings of the rishis of India that even today comprise the Eternal Dharma, that goes far beyond religion into realization.

In *The Christ of India* Swami Nirmalananda presents what those ancient teachings are, as well as the growing evidence that Jesus spent much of his "Lost Years" in India and Tibet. This is also the story of how the original teachings of Jesus and Saint Thomas thrived in India for centuries before the coming of the European colonialists.

May a Christian Believe in Reincarnation?

Discover the real and surprising history of reincarnation and Christianity.

A growing number of people are open to the subject of past lives, and the belief in rebirth–reincarnation, metempsychosis, or transmigration–is commonplace. It often thought that belief in reincarnation and Christianity are incompatible. But is this really true? May a Christian believe in reincarnation? The answer may surprise you.

"Those needing evidence that a belief in reincarnation is in accordance with teachings of the Christ need look no further: Plainly laid out and explained in an intelligent manner from one who has spent his life on a Christ-like path of renunciation and prayer/meditation."—Christopher T. Cook

The Unknown Lives of Jesus and Mary
Compiled from Ancient Records and Mystical Revelations

"There are also many other things which Jesus did, the which, if they should be written every one, I suppose that even the world itself could not contain the books that should be written." (Gospel of Saint John, final verse)

You can discover much of those "many other things" in this unique compilation of ancient records and mystical revelations, which includes historical records of the lives of Jesus Christ and his Mother Mary that have been accepted and used by the Church since apostolic times. This treasury of little-known stories of Jesus' life will broaden the reader's understanding of what Christianity really was in its original form.

Robe of Light
An Esoteric Christian Cosmology

In *Robe of Light* Swami Nirmalananda explores the whys and wherefores of the mystery of creation. From the emanation of the worlds from the very Being of God, to the evolution of the souls to their ultimate destiny as perfected Sons of God, the ideal progression of creation is described. Since the rebellion of Lucifer and the fall of Adam and Eve from Paradise flawed the normal plan of evolution, a restoration was necessary. How this came about is the prime subject of this insightful study.

Moreover, what this means to aspirants for spiritual perfection is expounded, with a compelling knowledge of the scriptures and of the mystical traditions of East and West.

The Gospel of Thomas for Awakening
A Commentary on Jesus' Sayings as Recorded by the Apostle Thomas

When the Apostles dispersed to the various area of the world, Thomas travelled to India, where evidence shows Jesus spent his Lost Years, and which had been the source of the wisdom which he had brought to the "West."

The Christ that Saint Thomas quotes in this ancient text is quite different than the Christ presented by popular Christianity. Through his unique experience and study with both Christianity and Indian religion, Swami Nirmalananda clarifies the sometimes enigmatic sayings of Jesus in an informative and inspiring way.

The Odes of Solomon for Awakening
A Commentary on the Mystical Wisdom of the Earliest Christian Hymns and Poems

The Odes of Solomon is the earliest Christian hymn-book, and therefore one of the most important early Christian documents. Since they are mystical and esoteric, they teach and express the classical and universal mystical truths of Christianity, revealing a Christian perspective quite different than that of "Churchianity," and present the path of Christhood that all Christians are called to.

"Fresh and soothing, these 41 poems and hymns are beyond delightful! I deeply appreciate Abbot George Burke's useful and illuminating insight and find myself spiritually re-animated." –John Lawhn

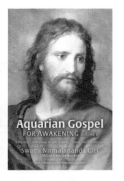

The Aquarian Gospel for Awakening (2 Volumes)
A Practical Commentary on Levi Dowling's Classic Life of Jesus Christ

Written in 1908 by the American mystic Levi Dowling, The Aquarian Gospel of Jesus the Christ answers many questions about Jesus' life that the Bible doesn't address. Dowling presents a universal message found at the heart of all valid religions, a broad vision of love and wisdom that will ring true with Christians who are attracted to Christ but put off by the narrow views of the tradition that has been given his name.

Swami Nirmalananda's commentary is a treasure-house of knowledge and insight that even further expands Dowling's vision of the true Christ and his message.

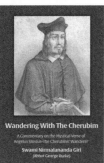

Wandering With The Cherubim
A Commentary on the Mystical Verse of Angelus Silesius–The Cherubinic Wanderer"

Johannes Scheffler, who wrote under the name Angelus Silesius, was a mystic and a poet. In his most famous book, "The Cherubinic Wanderer," he expressed his mystical vision.

Swami Nirmalananda reveals the timelessness of his mystical teachings and The Cherubinic Wanderer's practical value for spiritual seekers. He does this in an easily intelligible fashion for those wishing to put those priceless teachings into practice.

"Set yourself on the journey of this mystical poetry made accessible through this very beautifully commentated text. It is text that submerges one in the philosophical context of the Advaita notion of Non Duality. Swami Nirmalananda's commentary is indispensable in understanding higher philosophical ideas, for Swami's language, while readily approachable, is rich in deep essence of the teachings." –Savitri

The Dhammapada for Awakening
A Commentary on Buddha's Practical Wisdom

Swami Nirmalananda's commentary on this classic Buddhist scripture explores the Buddha's answers to the urgent questions, such as "How can I find find lasting peace, happiness and fulfillment that seems so elusive?" and "What can I do to avoid many of the miseries big and small that afflict all of us?" Drawing on his personal experience and on parallels in Hinduism and Christianity, the author sheds new light on the Buddha's eternal wisdom.

"Swami Nirmalananda's commentary is well crafted and stacked with anecdotes, humor, literary references and beautiful quotes from the Buddha. I found it to be entertaining as well as illuminating, and have come to consider it a guide to daily living."
–Rev. Gerry Nangle

The Tao Teh King for Awakening
A Practical Commentary on Lao Tzu's Classic Exposition of Taoism

"The Tao does all things, yet our interior disposition determines our success or failure in coming to knowledge of the unknowable Tao."

Lao Tzu's classic writing, the Tao Teh King, has fascinated scholars and seekers for centuries. His presentation of the Tao which is the Eternal Reality, and the Way of the Sage that is the path to the realization of and dwelling in this Reality is illuminating, but its deeper meanings and practical applications remain obscure to many, especially in the West.

Swami Nirmalananda offers a commentary that makes the treasures of Lao Tzu's teachings accessible and applicable for the sincere seeker.

More Titles

The Four Gospels for Awakening

Light on the Path for Awakening

How to Read the Tarot

Light from Eternal Lamps

Vivekachudamani: The Crest Jewel of Discrimination for Awakening

Magnetic Therapy: Healing in Your Hands

Made in United States
Cleveland, OH
27 December 2024

12757143R00059